Y0-CBA-863

SCRUGGS V. SNYDER

Second Edition

NITA Editorial Advisory Board

Kim J. Askew
Hughes & Luce, LLP
Dallas, Texas

Kenneth R. Feinberg
The Feinberg Group
Washington, D.C.

Lawrence I. Fox
McDermott Will & Emery
New York, New York

Jonathan S. Kagan
Irell & Manella, LLP
Los Angeles, California

Prof. Emeritus James W. McElhaney
Case Western Reserve University School of Law
Cleveland, Ohio

Jim M. Perdue
The Perdue Law Firm, LLP
Houston, Texas

Patricia Lee Refo
Snell & Wilmer, LLP
Phoenix, Arizona

Prof. Stephen A. Saltzburg
George Washington University Law School
Washington, D.C.

Hon. Deanell Reece Tacha
Chief Judge, U.S. Tenth Circuit
Lawrence, Kansas

~

Gregory J. Smith
NITA Director of Publications
Louisville, Colorado

Scruggs v. Snyder

Second Edition

William S. Bailey

Adjunct Professor
Seattle University School of Law

Frederick C. Moss

Associate Professor of Law
Dedman School of Law
Southern Methodist University

NATIONAL INSTITUTE FOR TRIAL ADVOCACY

© 2008 by the National Institute for Trial Advocacy

All rights reserved. No part of this work may be reproduced or transmitted in any form or by any means, electronic or mechanical, including photocopying and recording, or by any information storage or retrieval system without the prior written approval of the National Institute for Trial Advocacy unless such copying is expressly permitted by federal copyright law. Address inquiries to:

Reprint Permission
National Institute for Trial Advocacy
361 Centennial Parkway, Suite 220
Louisville, CO 80027
Phone: (800) 225-6482
Fax: (720) 890-7069
E-mail: permissions@nita.org

The video of the mock jury focus group was provided by Decision Quest and is reprinted on the accompanying DVD with permission.

ISBN: 978-1-60156-044-5

FBA: 1044

11 10 09 08   10 9 8 7 6 5 4 3 2 1

Manufactured in the United States of America

ACKNOWLEDGMENTS

The authors would like to acknowledge Aaron Weholt of Legal Media for his excellent work on the medical illustrations in this case file. Aaron can be contacted at aaron@legal-media.com or www.legal-media.com.

The authors would like to also thank our trial advocacy students and faculty who tried or judged mock jury trials of earlier versions of this case file and who made many valuable contributions to the file and suggestions on how to improve it.

The authors would also like to thank Shane Read for the use of his jury focus group video, borrowed from his companion book *Winning at Trial*.

TABLE OF CONTENTS

·

Newcomb's Diagrams, Computer Animation Stills, and Photograph

Medical Illustrations

Depositions of Potential Witnesses

DVD Contents

Pleadings

Exhibits

Depositions

Medical Reports

Treatise Excerpts

Jury Instructions

Verdict Forms

Newcomb's Computer Simulations

Defendant's Sequential Photo Study

Plaintiffs' Camp and Accident Scene Video[*]

Video of Mock Jury Focus Group[*]

---

[*] Note that this video requires DVD software to play.

SECTION I
CASE FILE

INTRODUCTION

This is a personal injury case involving a six-year-old child who ran across a busy highway while his family was staying at a state park over a July weekend. A number of motorists, including the defendant who hit the child, noticed him fidgeting by the fog line of the road just before he attempted to dash across it. A southbound truck pulling a boat trailer in the lane closest to the boy was able to slow down enough to avoid hitting him. The defendant, Lynn Snyder, who was coming in the other direction, hit the boy with the right front of Snyder's rental car.

The child, Sam Scruggs, survived with broken legs and a closed head injury. His parents claim that he suffered residual mental impairment as a result of the collision. The parents have brought this action against the defendant, alleging that the defendant failed to keep a proper lookout and was going too fast for the conditions. If the trial includes the issue of damages in addition to the liability issue, the only question that is presented to the jury is whether Sam suffered the impairment of his mental capacities. Money damages, if any, are not before the jury.

Defendant denies any negligence on his/her part and claims that the child suffered no lasting injury or impairment from the accident. The state highway patrol officer who investigated the accident determined that while the defendant had been drinking earlier in the day, Snyder was not over the legal blood alcohol limit and could not have done anything to avoid the accident. However, plaintiffs' accident reconstruction expert and an eyewitness state that there was enough time for the defendant to have avoided hitting the child if Snyder had not been talking on the phone and had reaction time slowed by alcohol.

Under Nita law, the six-year-old victim cannot be negligent. However, defendant alleges that the child was being improperly supervised by his parents, who negligently put the child under the supervision of his fifteen-year-old sibling, Robin. While the parents remained at their campsite some distance away, Robin's diverted attention at a softball game allowed Sam to slip off unnoticed and attempt to cross the busy road by himself.

Both sides rely heavily on demonstrative evidence. Plaintiffs have a video "walk through" of the camp and accident sites and three computer animations, which show there was enough time for the defendant to react, brake, and avoid hitting the child. Defendant relies upon a series of stop-action photographs taken by a state patrol officer that show that oncoming traffic blocked the defendant's view of the child when he dashed across the road so that the defendant could not see the child in time to avoid him.

The plaintiffs rely on the testimony of an expert neuropsychologist to prove that Sam suffered a closed head injury in the accident, with permanent residual effects. In support of this, plaintiffs have color medical illustrations of the affected areas of the brain. These illustrations describe the function of the frontal lobes. Plaintiffs argue that the frontal lobes of Sam's brain were damaged by the force of this collision. The plaintiffs' medical illustrations also describe the actual physical mechanism of the injury. This is available in both a conventional format, as well as in PowerPoint® with motion of the head and brain demonstrated.

The defendant has comparable color medical illustrations for use with the testimony of defendant's expert neuropsychologist, who will testify that Sam did not suffer any permanent cognitive or executive function impairment. One shows the normal CT scans of Sam's brain. The other shows the protections surrounding the brain that prevented any lasting harm to Sam. This illustration is available in both a conventional format, as well as in PowerPoint®, with motion and sequential text.

The computer has expanded greatly the visual resources available to the lawyer in the twenty-first century. Expert witnesses are much more compelling when they are able to "show and tell" during testimony. This case file attempts to familiarize the student with the latest, most sophisticated forms of visual evidence.

SPECIAL INSTRUCTIONS AND STIPULATIONS FOR USE AS A FULL TRIAL

When this case is used for a full trial on both liability and damages, the parties are limited to calling the following witnesses:

Chris Buck

Trooper Sandy Fielder

Alex Flyberg

Dr. Faridah Z. Goldhammer

Dr. H. Jan McClaren

Jan Moriarity

Dale Newcomb

Pat or Tammy Scruggs

Robin Scruggs

Lynn Snyder

If the case is tried on liability only, Drs. McClaren and Goldhammer are not necessary and should not be called as witnesses. All of the witnesses and parties can be of either gender. Only one of the Scruggs parents may be called. Any witness can be called by either party.

Note: When dates are given, years are expressed as "*[X yrs ago]*," with "X" being the number of years prior to the present year. For example, if the trial were held in 2008, then counsel and witnesses should refer to, "July 11, *[2 yrs ago]*," as "July 11, *2006*." The current year is written, "*[this yr]*."

Required Stipulations:

1. The laws of the State of Nita govern the trial of this case. The applicable laws are contained in the proposed jury instructions that are set forth at the end of the case. There is no issue of jurisdiction, venue, service of process, or propriety of the parties.

2. The date of the accident, July 11, was a Sunday.

3. The State of Nita was on Daylight Savings Time on the day of the accident.

4. The passenger in the defendant's car at the time of the accident, Divindra Patel, has returned to his/her home in India and could not afford to return to the United States for deposition or trial.

5. Divindra Patel is the same gender as Lynn Snyder.

6. Defense counsel may substitute an actual dark blue child's T-shirt for use at the trial in lieu of Exhibit 8, a picture of the dark blue T-shirt Sam Scruggs was wearing when hit. Plaintiffs may not contest its authenticity.

7. Plaintiffs' counsel may substitute a real pair of striped gray athletic shorts in lieu of Exhibit 9 as the shorts Sam Scruggs was wearing when hit. Defendant may not contest its authenticity.

8. A real, hand-lettered, roughly 8" × 10" sign may be substituted for Exhibit 10 if it is agreed to by both parties.

9. The trial judge has taken judicial notice that *Accident Reconstruction Principles* by Louis R. Charles and *Diagnosing Closed Head Injuries* by Wilbert Von Bulow qualify as "learned treatises" under Nita Rule of Evidence 803(18). Excerpts are in this file and are authentic.

10. The Nita Rules of Evidence and Procedure are identical to the Federal Rules of Evidence and Procedure except cross-examination is not limited to the scope of direct examination.

11. The statements made in the summarized depositions are admissible to the same extent as statements from full depositions.

12. Each witness must admit that the signature on his or her deposition is his or hers.

13. A pre-trial hearing was held on the parties' challenges to all of the experts' qualifications and the admissibility of their opinions under *Daubert*. The trial court ruled that all of the experts were qualified and may render their opinions and that Newcomb's computer animations and Trooper Fielder's stop-action photographs are admissible.

14. Multiplying the miles per hour a vehicle is traveling times 1.47 will give the feet per second that vehicle is traveling.

15. It is not illegal in the State of Nita to drive a motor vehicle while talking on a cell phone.

16. The Nita Supreme Court has abolished the common law "sudden emergency" doctrine.

17. Nita is a "pure" comparative negligence state. That is, a plaintiff can recover damages in proportion to the defendant's percentage of negligence even if plaintiff's negligence exceeds defendant's.

18. Nita law adopts the "Tender Years" doctrine whereby a child under the age of seven cannot be negligent or contributorily negligent.

19. The Supreme Court of Nita has held that the members of a family can be found negligent for placing a family member in the custody and care of another family member. Also, the Court

has held that negligence of this nature can be used by a third party in defense against the claims of the family member who was placed in the care and custody of another family member.

20. The Nita common law of torts provides that when parents place a child into the custody of another, whether a member of the family or not, the custodian is the agent of the parents and the negligence of the custodian is attributable to the parents. The negligence of the custodian may be claimed to be contributory negligence in defense against the claims of the child placed in the care of the custodian. The plaintiffs concede that Robin was acting as the parents' agent while Sam was in her custody and care.

21. Nita has no statute or common law doctrine requiring the driver of a motor vehicle to exercise *extraordinary* care upon seeing a child by the side of the road.

22. The trial court has ruled pretrial that it will not instruct the jury on "unavoidable accident."

23. When the trial includes the issue of damages as well as liability, the court has ruled that it will not hear evidence on the amount of money damages the plaintiffs are due, if any. The only issue for the finder of fact will be whether Sam Scruggs suffered an impairment of his cognitive functioning as a result of the accident (Question No. 6 on the Alternate Verdict Form). Thus, no evidence may be offered regarding pain and suffering; doctor, hospital, and rehabilitation costs both past and future; and Sam Scruggs' lost future earnings as a result of his alleged impairment. Thus, the damages part of the trial is limited to whether Sam suffers from a cognitive impairment as a result of the accident.

24. The video recorded "walk through" of the accident scene on the accompanying DVD that is referred to in some witness depositions was recorded by Paul Drake, an investigator for the plaintiffs' lawyer, around 1:30 p.m. on June 15, *[1 yr ago]*, eleven months after the accident.

IN THE CIRCUIT COURT OF
DARROW COUNTY, NITA
CIVIL DIVISION

PAT AND TAMMY SCRUGGS, married persons, as co-guardians of SAMUEL SCRUGGS, a minor,	))))	CIVIL ACTION CA 01970
Plaintiffs	))	
v.	))	COMPLAINT
LYNN SNYDER,	))	
Defendant.	)	

COME NOW the plaintiffs, Pat and Tammy Scruggs, husband and wife, as the duly appointed guardians of their minor son, Samuel Scruggs, against defendant, Lynn Snyder, and state and allege as follows:

I.   PARTIES AND JURISDICTION

1.1   Plaintiffs reside in Darrow County, Nita.

1.2   The material events and tortious conduct alleged herein occurred in Darrow County, Nita.

1.3   Defendant Lynn Snyder is believed to be a resident of the state of Massachusetts.

1.4   Jurisdiction and venue properly exist in the Circuit Court of the State of Nita, in and for Darrow County.

II.   FACTS

2.1   On or about July 11, *[2 yrs ago]*, plaintiffs were camping at Bayview State Park, Nita.

2.2   For unknown reasons, plaintiff Samuel Scruggs attempted to cross the Sun Coast Highway, which is adjacent to the baseball field at Bayview State Park.

2.3   Defendant was driving an automobile northbound the on Sun Coast Highway. Defendant failed to keep a proper lookout, traveling at an excessive speed for the conditions, and negligently operated his/her vehicle in such a manner as to collide with plaintiff Samuel Scruggs, causing permanent and debilitating injuries.

III. LIABILITY

3.1   As a direct and proximate result of the negligence of the defendant, Samuel Scruggs sustained permanent physical and mental injuries, including mental and physical pain, suffering, disability, and loss of enjoyment of life.

IV. PRAYER

WHEREFORE, plaintiffs pray for relief as follows:

4.1   For judgment against the defendant for general and special damages suffered by Samuel Scruggs in an amount to be determined at trial,

4.2   For plaintiffs' taxable costs and attorney's fees incurred herein,

4.3   For such other and further relief as the Court deems just.

DATED this 30th day of January *[1 yr ago]*.

Respectfully submitted,

JACOB BROOM
Attorney at Law
500 Delaware Building
Nita City, Nita

IN THE CIRCUIT COURT OF
DARROW COUNTY, NITA
CIVIL DIVISION

PAT AND TAMMY SCRUGGS, married persons, as co-guardians of SAMUEL SCRUGGS, a minor,	))))	CIVIL ACTION CA 01970
Plaintiffs	))	
v.	))	DEFENDANT'S ANSWER
LYNN SNYDER,	))	
Defendant.	)	

COMES NOW the defendant, Lynn Snyder, by and through his/her attorney, R. Carrie Smoke, and makes the following answer and affirmative defenses to the allegations in plaintiffs' Complaint:

I. ANSWER

1.1 For answer to the allegations contained in paragraph 1.1 of plaintiffs' Complaint, the same are admitted.

1.2 For answer to the allegations contained in paragraph 1.2 of plaintiffs' Complaint, the defendant making this answer denies any allegations of tortious conduct. Defendant admits that an incident occurred in Darrow County on July 11, *[2 yrs ago]*.

1.3 For answer to the allegations contained in paragraph 1.3 of plaintiffs' Complaint, defendant Snyder is a resident of Massachusetts.

1.4 For answer to the allegations contained in paragraph 1.4 of plaintiffs' Complaint, defendant is without sufficient information to form a belief as to the truth or falsity and as such, the same are denied.

NATIONAL INSTITUTE FOR TRIAL ADVOCACY

2.1 For answer to the allegations contained in paragraph 2.1 of plaintiffs' Complaint, defendant is without sufficient information to form a belief as to the truth or falsity and as such, the same are denied.

2.2 For answer to the allegations contained in paragraph 2.2 of plaintiffs' Complaint, defendant is without sufficient information to form a belief as to the truth or falsity and as such, the same are denied.

2.3 For answer to the allegations contained in paragraph 2.3 of plaintiffs' Complaint, defendant making this answer denies any allegations of tortious conduct and is without sufficient information to form a belief as to the truth or falsity of the remainder of the allegations and as such, the same are denied.

3.1 For answer to the allegations contained in paragraph 3.1 of plaintiffs' Complaint, defendant making this answer denies any allegations of tortious conduct. All allegations contained in this paragraph are denied.

II. AFFIRMATIVE DEFENSES

Further and by way of affirmative defenses, defendant Snyder alleges:

2.1 Samuel Scruggs' injuries, if any, were proximately caused by the negligence of his parents, Tammy and Pat Scruggs, who failed to exercise reasonable care for his safety.

2.2 Samuel Scruggs' injuries, if any, were proximately caused by the negligence of a third person, Robin Scruggs, who failed to exercise reasonable care for his safety and who was an agent of Tammy and Pat Scruggs.

WHEREFORE, having fully answered the allegations contained in plaintiffs' Complaint, defendant prays for the following relief:

1. That plaintiffs' Complaint be dismissed with prejudice and the plaintiffs take nothing thereby;

2. That in the event the plaintiffs recover a judgment against this answering defendant, that the judgment be reduced by the percentage of fault attributable to the

tortious conduct of Tammy and Pat Scruggs and/or Robin Scruggs, a third person for whose negligence Tammy and Pat Scruggs are responsible.

3.   That defendant be awarded costs and attorney's fees; and

4.   That defendant be granted such further relief as the Court deems just and equitable.

DATED this 21st day of February *[1 yr ago]*.

Respectfully submitted,

Carrie Smoke

R. CARRIE SMOKE
Attorney for the Defendant
2000 Uptown Tower
Nita City, Nita

NITA STATE PATROL
REPORT OF INVESTIGATION

Date/Time Reported: July 11, *[2 yrs ago]*, 1300 hrs.

Date/Time of Investigation: July 11, *[2 yrs ago]*, 1319–1530 hrs.

Name of Reporting Trooper: Sandy Fielder, Badge 521, Unit 0808

Location of Incident/Investigation: Sun Coast Highway, Milepost 56,
                                     Bayview State Park

Conditions: Weather: clear, sunny
                                     Road: dry
                                     Visibility: excellent
                                     Traffic: moderately heavy

Driver No. 1:   Lynn Snyder
                                     220 Maple St., Brookline, Mass.
                                     Height: 5' 9"
                                     Weight: 135 lbs
                                     Age: 27
                                     Occupation: Graduate student, Nita U.

Victim No. 1:   Sam Scruggs
                                     2227 Flagler Rd., Matlock, Nita
                                     Sex: M
                                     Height: 3' 11"
                                     Weight: 44 lbs
                                     Age: 6

Witnesses:

    No. 1   Alex Flyberg
                                     1829 Locust Ave., Nita City, Nita
    No. 2   Chris Buck ·
                                     1708 Vista Drive, Nita City, Nita
    No. 3   Jan Moriarity
                                     6016 Town Rd., Shell Beach, Nita
    No. 4   Pat Scruggs
                                     2227 Flagler Rd., Matlock, Nita
    No. 5   Divindra Patel
                                     314 Sonic Blvd., Nita City (Nita U. grad student
                                     from India)

NATIONAL INSTITUTE FOR TRIAL ADVOCACY

DETAILS OF INVESTIGATION

7/11/[2 yrs ago]; 1304 hrs: Dispatched to car-pedestrian accident on Sun Coast Hwy in Bay-view State Park. At scene 1319 hrs. Darrow Co. Sheriff directing traffic. NSP Sergeant Meyers in charge; requested I take photos, interview witnesses, measure skids and vehicles, and file accident report.

Victim #1 on shoulder of rd; conscious; poss broken legs. EMT arrived 1320 hrs. Interviewed witnesses. W#1 said was driving south on S.C. Hwy towing trailer w/ boat. V#1 appeared at shoulder, west side of road. V#1 paused, then ran in front of W#1's truck. W#1 dynamited brakes, missed V#1. V#1 continued across rd and was hit by Kia sedan driven by D#1 who also hit brakes. V#1 thrown into air, landing on shoulder. Not hit again. Ws ## 2, 3, 5 all describe the same. W#5 was passenger in Kia.

Interviewed Driver#1 at scene. D#1 said was driving with traffic flow, approx. 35 mph. Saw V#1 at side of rd, then dart in front of truck. D#1 slammed brakes, could not swerve. V#1 hit right front of Kia. Car damage to rt hood and rt side of front lic plate. Car new rental (Thrifty). Brakes, tires, windshield all good condition. D#1 said did not have lights on, not needed.

Smelled alcohol on D#1. Administered 3 standard field sobriety tests (H–T, F–N, Backward Count—all passed) before having D#1 blow into Alco-Sensor III. Test result = .07 BAC. No arrest.

Measured location of Kia and W#1's truck and their skidmarks after driving PK nails in pavement. Measured Kia. See addendum report. Took photos of scene. Attached.

No citations issued. Will return to scene tomorrow to do follow-up visibility tests and photos to determine D#1's opportunity/ability to see V#1 in sufficient time to avoid the accident.

Sandy Fielder

Investigating Officer
Badge No. _521_
Unit: _0808_
Report Date: _7/11/[2yrs ago]_

NITA STATE PATROL
REPORT OF INVESTIGATION

Addendum to: Report of S. Fielder, #521, Ped/Veh collision, 7/11/*[2 yrs ago]*, Sun Coast Hwy, 1300 hrs. Report of measurements

Filed: 7/11/*[2 yrs ago]*, 1615 hrs

Vehicle # 1:   Driver: Lynn Snyder

    Yr: *[2 yrs ago]* Make: Kia Model: Sephia   Style: 4-dr   Lic #: 947-GQY (WA)
    Owner: Thrifty Rental   Mileage: 4,731   Color: blue

    Overall length: 8' 3" Frt axle-frt bmpr: 2' 11"   Rear axle-rear bmpr: 2' 11"
    Width: 5' 5"

Brakes: ok   Steering: ok   Tire pressure: ok   Lights: n/a

Skid Marks:

    Reference Points: PK spike driven into west edge of road & west edge fog line.

    Vehicle #1: length right skid = 64' 11";   length left skid = 59' 4"
        end of skid marks to where front tires came to rest = 29'
        [Note: Other skid mark measurements have been omitted]

    Vehicle #2: Driver: A. Flyberg (witness) (Pickup hauling boat on trailer)

    Reference Points: Same as for Vehicle #1

    Length of right skid = 104' 7"   Length of left skid = 126' 5"
    [Note: Other skid mark measurements have been omitted.]

Road Width: 36' 1" fog line to fog line. Center line: 13' from east edge

Reporting Officer: S. Fielder, #521

EXHIBIT 1

WIDE AERIAL PHOTO OF ACCIDENT SCENE

EXHIBIT 1A

Exhibit 1A

WIDE AERIAL PHOTO OF ACCIDENT SCENE (UNMARKED)

EXHIBIT 2

PHOTO OF SKID MARKS OF TRUCK AND KIA

EXHIBIT 2A

Exhibit 2A

PHOTO OF SKID MARKS OF TRUCK AND KIA (UNMARKED)

EXHIBIT 3

PHOTO OF POINT OF IMPACT

EXHIBIT 3A

Exhibit 3A

PHOTO OF POINT OF IMPACT (UNMARKED)

EXHIBIT 4

Exhibit 4

PHOTO OF TRUCK SKID

Exhibit 4A

Exhibit 4A

PHOTO OF TRUCK SKID (UNMARKED)

EXHIBIT 5

PHOTO OF TRAFFIC

Exhibit 6

Photo of Pedestrian Tunnel Entrance

EXHIBIT 7

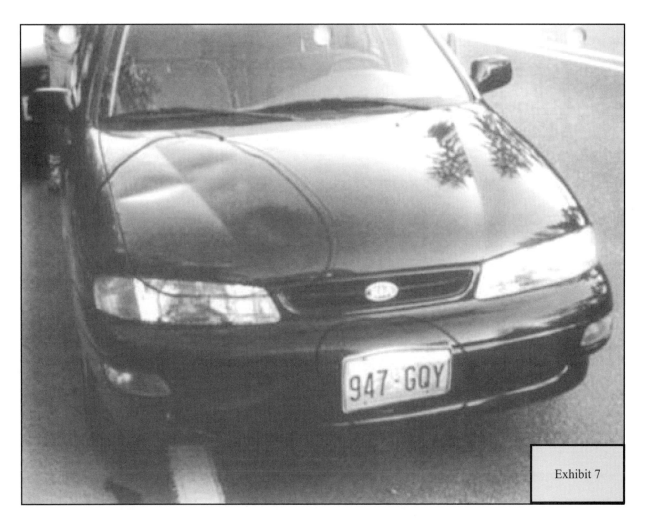

Exhibit 7

PHOTO OF DAMAGE TO KIA

EXHIBIT 7A

Exhibit 7A

PHOTO OF DAMAGE TO KIA (UNMARKED)

EXHIBIT 8

Exhibit 8

PHOTO OF SAM'S T-SHIRT

EXHIBIT 9

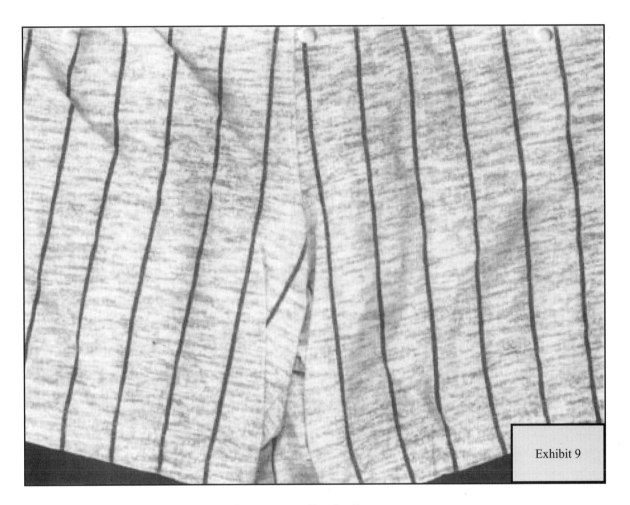

Exhibit 9

PHOTO OF SAM'S SHORTS

EXHIBIT 10

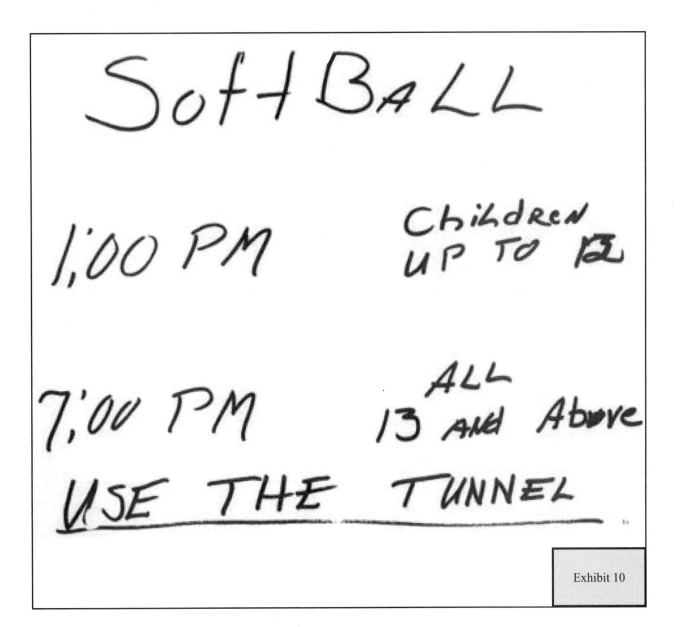

Exhibit 10

PHOTO OF SIGN FOR SOFTBALL GAME

EXHIBIT 11

Exhibit 11A

Exhibit 11B

PHOTOS OF SIGN FOR PEDESTRIAN UNDERPASS AND BALL FIELDS

EXHIBIT 12

Exhibit 12

PHOTO OF HIGHWAY FROM EAST SIDE

Exhibit 13

Exhibit 13

PHOTO OF UNDERPASS ENTRY FROM CAMPGROUND

Exhibit 14

Exhibit 14

Photo of Underpass Entry from West of Highway

EXHIBIT 15

Exhibit 15

PHOTO OF HILL BETWEEN BACKSTOP AND UNDERPASS ENTRY

EXHIBIT 16

Exhibit 16A

Exhibit 16B

PHOTOS OF WEST UNDERPASS ENTRY

Exhibit 17

Exhibit 17

Photo of Steps to Ball Field

EXHIBIT 18

PHOTO OF UNDERPASS

EXHIBIT 19

Exhibit 19

PHOTO OF UNDERPASS

EXHIBIT 20

Exhibit 20

PHOTO OF SAM'S CLOTHING WITH STAND-IN

EXHIBIT 21

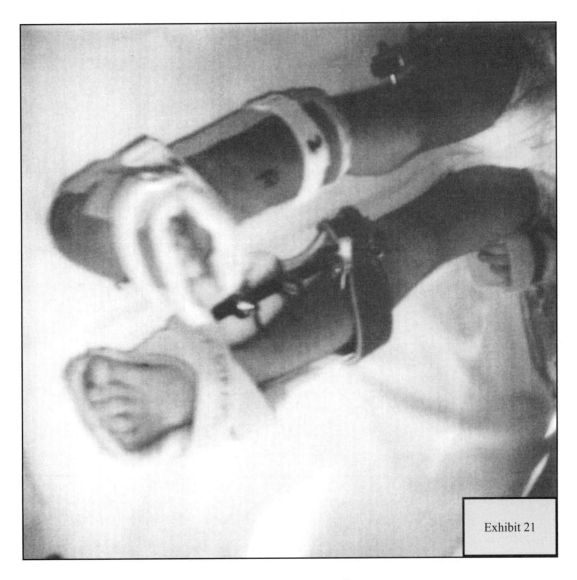

Exhibit 21

PHOTO OF SAM'S LEG BRACES

Exhibit 22

Exhibit 22

Defendant's Sequential Photo Study A

EXHIBIT 23

Exhibit 23

DEFENDANT'S SEQUENTIAL PHOTO STUDY B

EXHIBIT 24

Exhibit 24

DEFENDANT'S SEQUENTIAL PHOTO STUDY C

EXHIBIT 25

Exhibit 25

DEFENDANT'S SEQUENTIAL PHOTO STUDY D

EXHIBIT 26

Exhibit 26

DEFENDANT'S SEQUENTIAL PHOTO STUDY E

EXHIBIT 27

Exhibit 27

DEFENDANT'S SEQUENTIAL PHOTO STUDY F

EXHIBIT 28

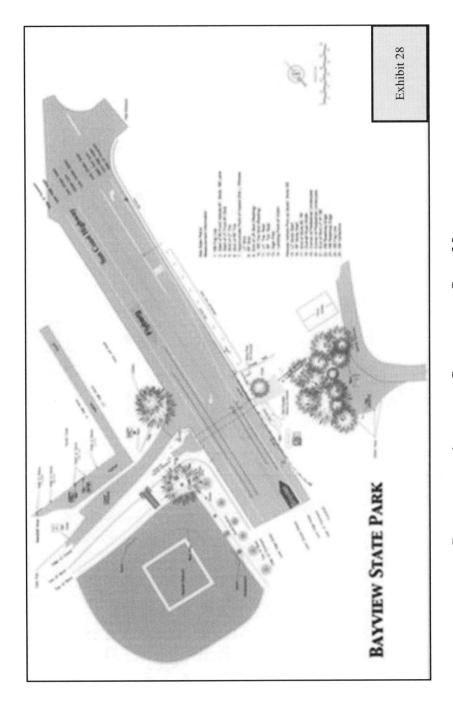

Exhibit 28A

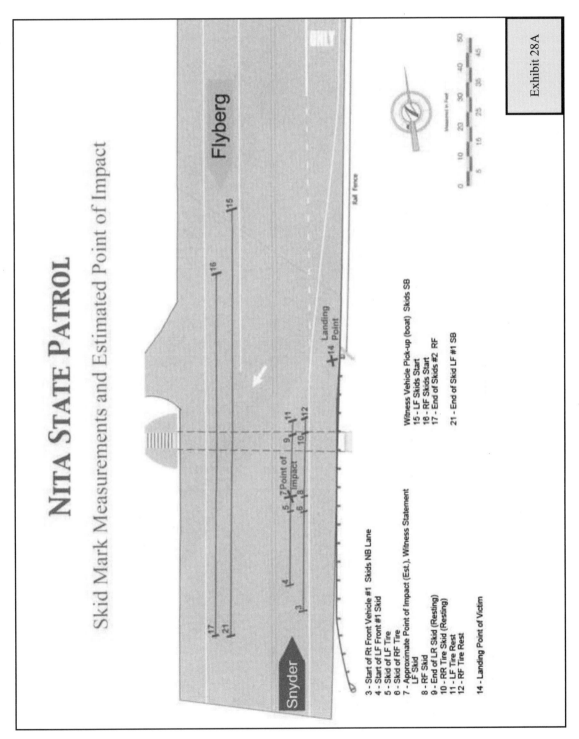

Close Up of Diagram of Accident Scene with Skid Marks

EXHIBIT 29

Exhibit 29

CHILD NEARS THE EDGE OF THE ROAD. KIA IS APPROXIMATELY 275' AWAY.

EXHIBIT 30

Exhibit 30

CHILD PAUSING AT THE EDGE OF THE ROAD. KIA IS APPROXIMATELY 200' AWAY.

EXHIBIT 31

Exhibit 31

CHILD CLEARS THE PATH OF THE TRUCK. KIA IS APPROXIMATELY 90' AWAY.

Exhibit 32

Exhibit 32

CHILD AT CENTER OF ROAD. KIA BEGINS BRAKING, APPROXIMATELY 40' AWAY.

EXHIBIT 33

Exhibit 33

KIA IMPACTING CHILD.

EXHIBIT 34

PHOTO OF PEDESTRIAN 53' FROM CAR

EXHIBIT 35

Anatomy and Functional Areas of the Brain

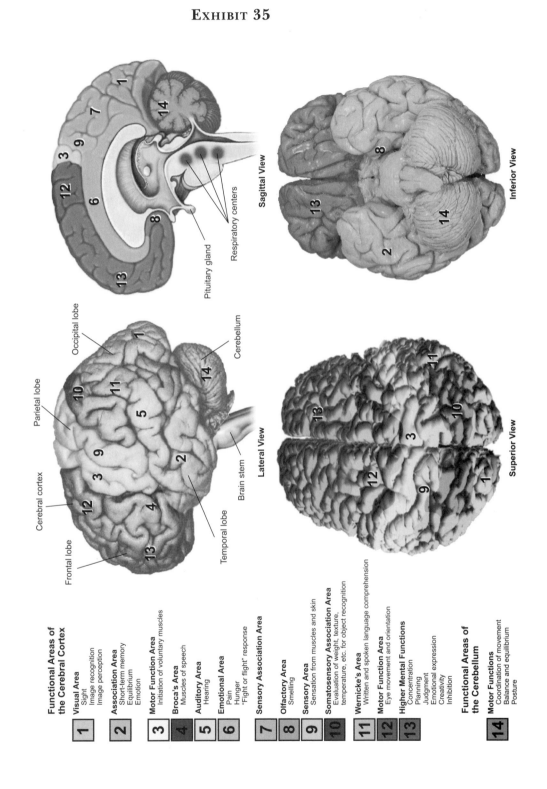

Functional Areas of the Cerebral Cortex

1 **Visual Area**
Sight
Image recognition
Image perception

2 **Association Area**
Short-term memory
Equilibrium
Emotion

3 **Motor Function Area**
Initiation of voluntary muscles

4 **Broca's Area**
Muscles of speech

5 **Auditory Area**
Hearing

6 **Emotional Area**
Pain
Hunger
"Fight or flight" response

7 **Sensory Association Area**

8 **Olfactory Area**
Smelling

9 **Sensory Area**
Sensation from muscles and skin

10 **Somatosensory Association Area**
Evaluation of weight, texture,
temperature, etc. for object recognition

11 **Wernicke's Area**
Written and spoken language comprehension

12 **Motor Function Area**
Eye movement and orientation

13 **Higher Mental Functions**
Concentration
Planning
Judgment
Emotional expression
Creativity
Inhibition

Functional Areas of the Cerebellum

14 **Motor Functions**
Coordination of movement
Balance and equilibrium
Posture

99

EXHIBIT 36

The Purpose of the Frontal Lobes . . .

Control of Higher Mental Functions

Concentration
Planning
Judgment
Emotional expression
Creativity
Inhibition

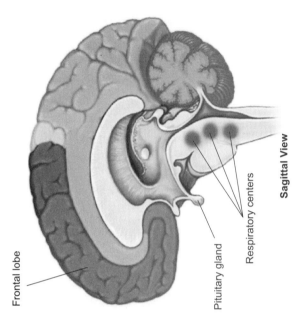

Frontal lobe

Pituitary gland

Respiratory centers

Sagittal View

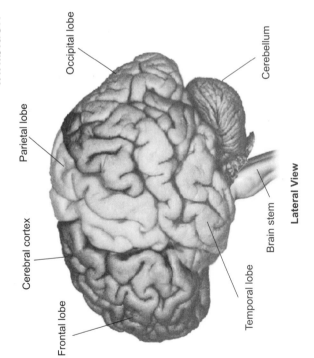

Occipital lobe

Cerebellum

Parietal lobe

Cerebral cortex

Brain stem

Lateral View

Frontal lobe

Temporal lobe

EXHIBIT 37

Close-up Views of Traumatic Brain Injury

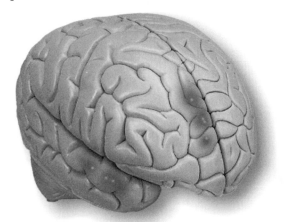

View of damaged frontal brain tissue after impact

Front

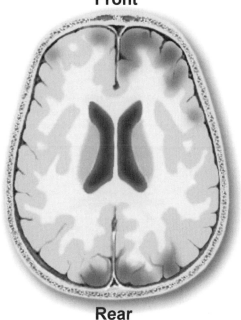

Rear

**Cross section showing damage to
front & rear brain tissue after impact**

EXHIBIT 38

Sam Scruggs
Mechanism of Head Injury

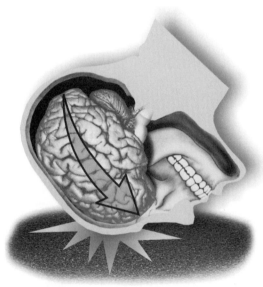

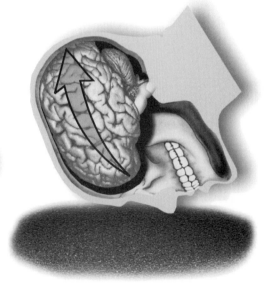

**Front (anterior aspect) of brain
impacts cranial wall when
Sam Scruggs strikes the road**

**Rebound - Rear (posterior aspect)
of brain impacts cranial wall**

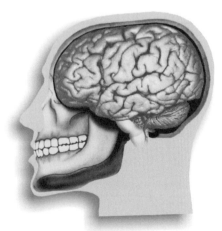

Front and rear of brain are damaged

EXHIBIT 39A

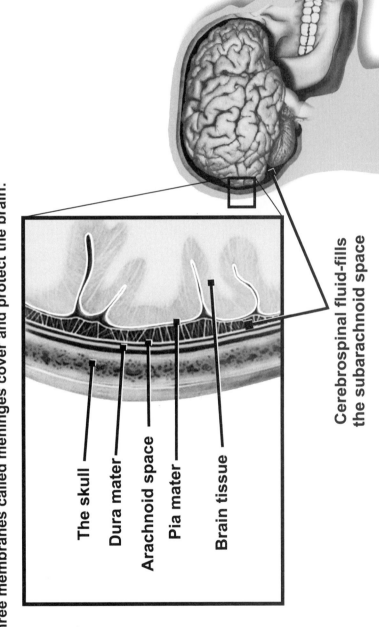

THE BRAIN IS WELL PROTECTED

Three membranes called meninges cover and protect the brain:

The skull

Dura mater

Arachnoid space

Pia mater

Brain tissue

Cerebrospinal fluid-fills the subarachnoid space

Exhibit 39B

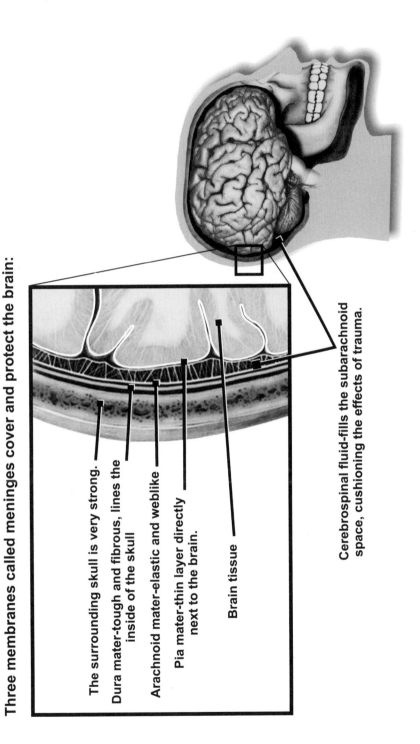

THE BRAIN IS WELL PROTECTED

Three membranes called meninges cover and protect the brain:

The surrounding skull is very strong.

Dura mater-tough and fibrous, lines the inside of the skull

Arachnoid mater-elastic and weblike

Pia mater-thin layer directly next to the brain.

Brain tissue

Cerebrospinal fluid-fills the subarachnoid space, cushioning the effects of trauma.

Exhibit 40A

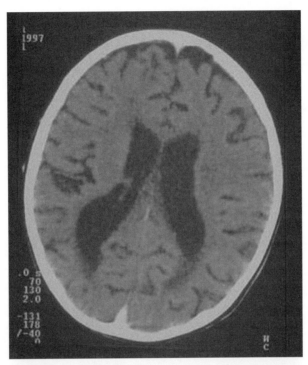

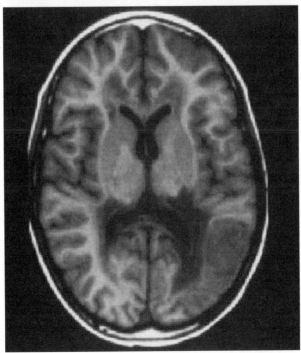

Sam's Postaccident Brain Scans

Exhibit 40B

Sam's Postaccident Brain Scans Were Normal

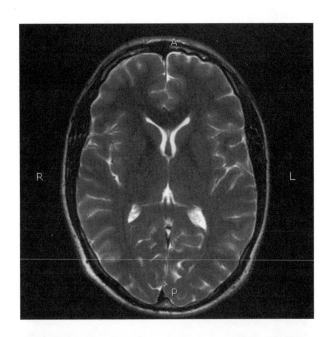

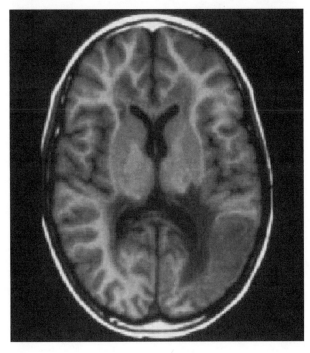

Deposition of Chris Buck

July 25, *[1 yr ago]*

1   My name is Chris Buck. I live at 1708 Vista Drive, Nita City, Nita. I am forty-five years old. I have
2   worked for the U.S. Postal Service for twenty years. I am a supervisor at the North Nita City station.
3   I have about a dozen people who work under me.

4   I was a witness to the pedestrian-car accident on the Sun Coast Highway in Bayview State Park a
5   year ago, Sunday, July 11, *[2 yrs ago]*, around 1:00 p.m. I was alone in my car. My spouse and I were
6   having some neighbors over to the house that evening for barbeque. We ran out of barbeque sauce,
7   and I didn't have enough ice cream for dessert since a couple more folks showed up than I had planned
8   for. I was on the way to a small grocery just up the road from the accident. It is where a lot of park
9   campers shop.

10   I was headed southbound on the Sun Coast Highway. Traffic was not heavy—lots of cars, camp-
11 ers, and pickups—but we were moving right along, with several car lengths between us—both ways.
12 The photo marked Exhibit 5 is a good illustration of how the traffic was that day. It was a week after
13 the Fourth of July holiday. Also, it was early in the day for people to be headed home yet. The weather
14 was clear. It was a beautiful, sunny day. The road was dry. A perfect day for visiting the park with your
15 family.

16   I'm quite familiar with that stretch of road. I travel it daily to and from work. Plus, living not far
17 away, I travel it all the time doing errands. I've lived at my current address for about eight years. Exhibit
18 2 is a good photo of the road where the accident took place.

19   I was driving my Subaru wagon around 45 mph, though the speed limit is 55. There was a steady
20 flow of traffic traveling 45-ish, but I usually drop my speed going through the park because it is a
21 somewhat dangerous area. Cars pull out from the nearby park entrance, and people walk across the
22 road and along the shoulder all the time on weekends when the park is crowded. Anyone familiar with
23 the park knows this.

24   There was a Ford pickup pulling a boat and trailer about five car lengths ahead of me. It was go-
25 ing the same speed as me, but I like to stay farther back from trailers than cars. I'm always afraid they
26 will come unattached or something will fly off them and through my windshield. Ahead of the pickup
27 with the boat, I believe there was just a line of cars. I seem to recall a couple of compacts in front of the
28 pickup. The first was five to eight car lengths ahead of the pickup. The cars were pulling away slightly
29 from the truck even though the road is level at that point. They weren't weighted down by the boat.

30   The accident was one of the most terrible and terrifying things I've ever seen. God knows why the
31 boy wasn't killed. I first saw the child who was hit coming up to the side of the road to my right. I was
32 probably 200 feet away from him. I couldn't tell at that point if it was a boy or girl, but the child was

1   young, about five to seven years old. There was a ball field backstop and some people at the top of the
2   hill above where he came from. The child must have come from there.

3   The child was coming up to the side of the road at a slight jogging speed and continued right to
4   the edge of the road about where the fog line is. At that point, I took my foot off of the gas and was
5   coasting—just in case. Exhibit 4 shows that hill to the right, as does Exhibit 5. He paused for only
6   a second or two, was looking both ways, up and down the road the whole time, and then crouched
7   slightly—like a sprinter in a race—and took off running directly across the road right in the path of
8   the pickup in front of me. My heart stopped! "Foolish, foolish child!" I cried out to myself.

9   The pickup slammed on its brakes, with screeching and smoke coming from its tires. I slammed on
10   my brakes too. I was sure the truck hit the kid. But an instant later I saw the boy sprint to the center
11   line of the road, pause for no more than a second, look at the oncoming northbound traffic, and sprint
12   into that lane of traffic.

13   There was a small foreign compact car headed for him in that lane. Later, I saw that it was a Kia.
14   I remember thinking, "He/she doesn't see the boy!" I thought this because the car had not begun to
15   brake until the boy began his sprint from the center line. Also, as I looked at the oncoming Kia, it
16   appeared to me that the driver—there were two persons in the car—was talking on a cell phone. I
17   couldn't actually see a phone, but it appeared that the driver's left hand was to his/her left ear. I didn't
18   notice anything about the passenger other than that there was one.

19   I thought the boy might get hit by the truck, but I was wrong. As the boy took off from the center
20   line, the Kia slammed on its brakes and started sliding toward the boy. Its front tires created a big cloud
21   of white smoke. Tragically, the Kia hit him, knocking him up onto the hood, and as the car stopped,
22   the boy was thrown another 100 feet or so onto the shoulder. I remember seeing one of his tennis shoes
23   fly off. Meanwhile, cars behind me and the Kia were all screeching to a stop; horns were blowing. I was
24   afraid I'd be rear-ended but I wasn't.

25   I pulled my car off the highway and ran to the boy. He was unconscious, but there was no real
26   blood except some scrapes. Several other witnesses and I called 911.

27   The driver of the Kia and his/her friend pulled over and came to see to the boy. The driver said
28   he/she did not see him until it was too late. I can't understand why. It seemed perfectly obvious that
29   the boy was going to try to cross the road. I didn't want to berate or argue with the driver at this point.
30   Our main concern was getting an ambulance there as quickly as possible. Still, I'll bet if that driver
31   wasn't on the phone, he/she would have seen the boy earlier. When I first saw the boy at the side of
32   the road, I have no doubt that I took my foot off the gas. I don't specifically remember. It is something
33   I'd do reflexively. After all, if I hadn't, I'd have eaten a boat for dinner that night. I also recall the Kia
34   passenger saying to the driver something like, "Forget catching a flight today."

35   The State Patrol and the Sheriff's Department arrived very quickly. It took longer for the ambu-
36   lance to get there. When they did, the boy was conscious. His parents showed up and were terribly
37   upset, as you can imagine. After a while, a state trooper spoke to me about what I saw. The trooper
38   took photos, talked to other witnesses, and measured things. I recall that after I mentioned to the State
39   Patrol Trooper that the Kia driver appeared to be on the phone, the Trooper asked the driver if he/
40   she had been on a cell phone at the time of the accident. The driver said no, that the passenger was. I

1 missed my dinner that night, but I couldn't eat when I got home. I was too upset. I'm so glad the boy

2 lived and, I've been told, is now back in school. That was nearly his last day on earth.

I have read the foregoing deposition and hereby affix my signature that the same is true and correct except as noted herein.

Chris Buck

———————————————————

Signature of Deponent

This deposition was taken in the office of defendant's counsel on July 25, *[1 yr ago]*. This deposition was given under oath and was read and signed by the deponent.

Certified by:

Penelope Harrison

———————————————————

Penelope Harrison
Certified Shorthand Reporter
(CSR)

DEPOSITION OF SANDY FIELDER

April 27, *[1 yr ago]*

1 My name is Sandy Fielder. I am thirty-one years old. I have been a Nita State Trooper for nine
2 years. I am married and have two children aged two and six. I live at 2345 Wood Glen Road in
3 Quiet Sound, Nita.

4 I grew up in Nita and have a bachelor's of science degree in criminal justice from Nita State
5 University. Upon graduation, I entered the Nita State Patrol's academy and graduated four months
6 later as a State Trooper. I've been working the Bayview State Park area for three years.

7 My duties include accident investigation, enforcing traffic laws, and assisting other law enforce-
8 ment agencies. I had a basic course in accident investigation at the State Patrol Academy. It dealt
9 with topics such as which law enforcement agencies have primary responsibility for handling high-
10 way accidents and what our duties at an accident are, such as traffic control, preservation of the
11 accident scene and evidence, learning about the various forms that have to be completed after an
12 accident (the accident report, field drawings, measurements, witness statement forms, etc.), how and
13 what to photograph, and things like that. We were not trained in reconstructing an accident. I've
14 handled only a few vehicle-pedestrian accidents in my nine years as a Trooper.

15 I was dispatched to the Scruggs' accident on July 11, *[2 yrs ago],* the Sunday after the July Fourth
16 weekend. I arrived shortly after 1:00 p.m. Other State Patrol and Darrow County Sheriff's Office
17 units were already there. Trooper Meyers was the primary officer on the scene. He asked me to com-
18 plete the accident report, speak to the witnesses, and do whatever measurements and photos that I
19 felt were needed to document the accident. He dealt with the injured boy and traffic control with
20 the Sheriff's deputies. The EMTs arrive about the same time I did.

21 When I arrived, the injured boy, Sam Scruggs, was lying on the shoulder of the road. He was
22 conscious but could not talk. He was crying and in great pain from multiple scrapes and bruises
23 and at least one, possibly two, broken legs. His sibling, Robin, was with him, and his parents arrived
24 shortly thereafter.

25 The car that hit the boy was driven by Lynn Snyder. It was on the side of the road where it
26 stopped after hitting the boy. The car was a new, rented Kia. There was one passenger, Divindra Pa-
27 tel. I spoke to both of them and several witnesses who saw the accident. I interviewed a Chris Buck,
28 Alex Flyberg, Jan Moriarity, and the parents of the injured boy, Pat and Tammy Scruggs.

29 According to witnesses, the Scruggs child, who was six years old, was hit by the Kia as he ran
30 across the Sun Coast Highway. All agreed that he ran from the west side of the highway toward the
31 east side. A truck pulling a boat in the southbound lane near where the boy entered the highway
32 slammed on its brakes and almost hit him. The truck was driven by Alex Flyberg. After almost

1 being hit, the boy continued across the road and was hit by Snyder's northbound Kia even though
2 Snyder slammed on the brakes. The boy was thrown in the air and landed on the east shoulder of the
3 highway. There was no sign that the Kia took evasive action other than braking. The Kia left clear skid
4 marks, as did the truck pulling the boat. The damage to the right front of the Kia indicated that Sny-
5 der almost missed him. Another split second and the boy would have cleared the car. The boy's sibling
6 and parents said that he had been at the ball field shortly before the accident. They didn't know why
7 he left alone and tried to cross the road rather than use the pedestrian underpass that was right there.

8 The posted speed limit at that point is 55 mph. Snyder told me that he/she was traveling at about
9 35–40 mph with the other cars in his/her line of traffic. Snyder said that there was no time to swerve
10 to avoid the child. Snyder said that he/she noticed a child standing by the edge of the road to his/her
11 left some distance ahead. The passenger, Patel, said that he/she did not notice the boy until he/she
12 heard the truck slam on its brakes. They were too close to him to stop. Snyder said that he/she had
13 hoped that the boy would stop at the center line and wait for the traffic to clear, but he didn't.

14 While interviewing the witnesses, one—Chris Buck, I think—told me that it appeared that
15 the driver of the Kia was talking on a cell phone when the boy entered the road. I inspected the
16 interior of the Kia and noticed a cell phone on the floor of the driver's side. I picked it up and
17 noticed that it was still connected to another number. I handed it to Patel, who said it was Sny-
18 der's but that Patel had been talking to the airline that Snyder had a flight on later that day. Patel
19 disconnected the call and handed the phone to Snyder. I asked Snyder if Snyder had been on the
20 phone, and Snyder denied it, saying that Patel was on the phone. Now that you have told me Sny-
21 der admits being on the phone when the accident occurred, I am less sure than I was before that
22 Snyder was not in part responsible for the accident. Obviously I'm concerned that I was lied to
23 and that the effects of both drinking and distraction may have been at work.

24 The weather was clear, dry, and sunny. Visibility was excellent. There is a double yellow line
25 down the center of the highway through the Park, so passing is not allowed.

26 The traffic that afternoon was moderately heavy in both directions. The heaviest traffic on
27 Sundays on the Sun Coast Highway through Bayview Park in the summer is in the morning and
28 evening, so the accident occurred before the traffic gets heavy. Exhibit 5 shows how the traffic was
29 when I got to the scene. It is possible that oncoming traffic could have obscured the child from
30 Snyder's view until he was in the road.

31 Bayview Park is somewhat unusual in that the busy Sun Coast Highway goes through the
32 middle of the park. This is a hazard if pedestrians try to cross the road, so they have a pedestrian
33 tunnel there. I don't know why the boy didn't use it. It is kind of dark and dank. He must have
34 been scared of it or in a hurry. Despite the underpass, I often see pedestrians cross the highway
35 there.

36 Families with children often come to this park to camp. Children as pedestrians definitely
37 raise safety concerns. Children don't have the judgment that adults do. They are more impulsive
38 and don't appreciate traffic dangers as much as adults.

39 I made no independent estimate of the speed of the Snyder vehicle. No one I spoke to at the
40 scene indicated that Snyder was speeding. Fifty-five is the posted speed limit along this part of the

1 highway. But, with all the campers, RVs, and towed boats on the road during the summer, I would
2 be surprised if anyone could ever exceed the speed limit. I give out very few speeding tickets in
3 that area on summer Sundays.

4 I drove marking nails, called PK nails, into the road at the point where each skid mark began
5 and ended. We do this because the marks can get washed away by rain, worn away by traffic, or
6 obscured by other skid marks later. We don't remove them later. I'd bet they are still there.

7 Trooper Devane and I then measured the skid marks of both the Kia and truck in relation to
8 a single PK-nail marked reference point, recording our results in the accident report. We created
9 this reference point on the white fog line on the west edge of the road and measured the distances
10 of the skid marks at various points to it. We don't just go onto the road and measure the length
11 of the skid marks with a tape in our investigations, as this would not tell us how much the skid
12 veered from one side to another. Not all skids are straight. Measuring in relation to our reference
13 point allowed us to map the lateral movement of the skidding Kia. Our measurements also would
14 allow a trained accident reconstruction expert to create a scale diagram map showing exactly
15 where the skid marks appeared on the road, as well as car speeds and other calculations. I am not
16 sufficiently trained to do this myself.

17 The skid marks left by the pickup pulling the boat were twice as long as those left by the Kia
18 sedan. The pickup's right skid mark was 104' 7" long; the left skid was 126' 5", whereas the Kia's
19 right skid was 64' 11" and left skid mark was 59' 4". This is what I would expect, because the
20 truck weighed more and was pulling a boat. A number of factors go into the length of a skid: the
21 weight of the vehicle, the roadway surface material, the condition of the surface (new, old, wet,
22 dry, etc.), the condition of the brakes and tires, and the speed of the vehicle. I am not able to
23 estimate the speed of the vehicle from the length of the skid marks. I made no calculations based
24 upon the data collected by my investigation. There was no need to, given what I was told by wit-
25 nesses and what I saw.

26 We are taught that the average reaction time is from 1.0 to 1.5 seconds. Though I didn't actu-
27 ally do the math, you could start from where Snyder's skid marks began and then back up another
28 1.0 to 1.5 seconds at the speed he/she was traveling. That would likely be Snyder's point of percep-
29 tion of the danger created by the pedestrian. That's when the reaction time begins—from seeing
30 and realizing the need to stop to getting your foot on the brake.

31 There is the possibility that Snyder's reaction time could have been slowed due to being on
32 the phone and by alcohol. I noticed the odor of alcohol on Snyder and the passenger, Patel.
33 They admitted to having some margaritas at lunch an hour or so earlier, so I administered a
34 series of field sobriety tests to see if Snyder was under the influence. We are trained at the acad-
35 emy how to perform these tests according to the standards of the National Highway Traffic
36 Safety Administration.

37 First, I administered the "walk and turn" test. I had Snyder move over to the fog line, place his/
38 her arms to his/her sides, and take nine steps heel-to-toe along the line. The subject then must turn
39 180 degrees on one foot and return in the same manner. Snyder lost his/her balance a couple times,
40 but because there was a slight tilt to the road at that point, I deemed the test inconclusive.

1   Then I administered the Romberg nose-touch test, having Snyder close his/her eyes, tilt his/
2 her head all the way back, hold his/her arms straight out to the sides, and touch his/her nose with
3 the index fingers. Snyder performed this well.

4   Then, I asked Snyder to count backward from seventy-three to sixty-one. Snyder passed.

5   Finally, since this was an injury accident, I was required by department policy to administer a
6 preliminary breath test with a portable breath tester called the Alco-Sensor III. This is a voluntary
7 test and Snyder agreed to take it.

8   I received a half day of training on the proper use of the Alco-Sensor I at the academy, and I had
9 a refresher course on the newest model, the Alco-Sensor III, only three months before this accident.
10 The device requires regular calibration and maintenance. The one I used that day had been serviced
11 and calibrated the previous week and had not been used since. I retrieved it from my car, turned it
12 on, and waited for it to indicate it was ready. The Alco-Sensor's temperature was within limits, and
13 after pushing the "read" button, it sampled the ambient air. The reading was below the 0.003 limit.
14 I made sure Snyder had nothing in his/her mouth and had not drunk any alcohol in the last fifteen
15 minutes, as required. (This test was at least thirty minutes after the accident). Snyder blew into the
16 plastic tube. The machine estimated that Snyder's blood alcohol level was .07. This is .01 under the
17 legal limit of .08 in Nita. Since Snyder seemed otherwise in good shape, I did not arrest Snyder or
18 issue a ticket, and let him/her leave in the Kia. Yes, I learned at the academy that a person's reac-
19 tion time is slowed by ingesting alcohol or drugs. It skews a driver's perceptions and judgment and
20 impairs their ability to react.

21   The following day, July 12, I returned to the scene with photographer Jan Short, a friend who is
22 a professional photographer, to take some pictures of the accident site and stop-action photographs
23 of the view that would have been available to the driver of the Kia. I had my six-year-old niece stand
24 by the side of the highway where I think Sam was standing. She is shown in Exhibit 20. My niece
25 was wearing clothes similar in color to those Sam Scruggs wore, that is, a dark blue T-shirt and grey
26 shorts. I used my personal Toyota Corolla instead of my patrol car because the driver's seat in the
27 Corolla was just about the same height as the driver's seat of the Kia. I wanted to get as close to the
28 same vantage point as possible.

29   It was about the same time of day when the accident happened, around 1:00 p.m. I approached
30 the scene driving northbound, just as Snyder had. The photographer was in the back seat holding
31 his camera next to my right ear. He took one picture per second of the view ahead as I drove about
32 40 mph. My niece was standing at the west side of the road near the pedestrian underpass where
33 witnesses said Sam was before running into the road. My niece was all but invisible at that point be-
34 cause her dark clothing blended in with the dark shadows of the trees behind her. Also, our view of
35 her was intermittently blocked by oncoming southbound cars. The photos were put on a CD in the
36 sequence taken. The photos on the CD accurately show what I saw from the driver's seat. Exhibits
37 22 through 27 are some of these photos.

38   Short and I also walked around the accident site and took a few photos. I had Short take photos
39 I thought showed some important features of the scene. I did not append them to my report since I
40 got them from Short after my report was filed. The first one, Exhibit 12, is from the east side of the

1   highway south of the point where the accident happened. You can see the backstop of the softball
2   field across the road and up the small hill. Exhibit 13 shows the entry to the underpass on the east
3   side of the road where the Scruggs family was camped. Exhibit 14 shows the entry to the pedestrian
4   underpass from the west side of the highway. The steps to the right lead up to the ball field. Exhibit
5   15 shows the small hill leading from the tree behind the backstop on the ball field to the underpass
6   entry on the west side of the road. The pictures in Exhibits 16A and 16B show the west-side entry
7   to the underpass. Exhibit 16A is taken from the top of the hill behind the backstop. Exhibit 17 is a
8   wide shot taken from the ball field showing the steps up to the field, the highway, the tree behind the
9   backstop, and the west-side entry to the underpass in the tree's shadow. Exhibits 18 and 19 are close-up
10 shots of the pedestrian underpass from the east side entrance.

11   My photos of the scene taken the day of the accident were attached to my accident report. The
12 exhibits I'm looking at now are identified as follows:

13   Exhibit 1A is an aerial view of the park that was in our office files. It accurately shows what the
14 accident location looked like at that time. Exhibit 1 is the view of the highway and the adjacent
15 recreational field blown up and printed. I marked on it roughly the direction that Flyberg's truck
16 and the Kia were driving, and roughly the point where Sam entered the road and his direction of
17 travel.

18   Exhibit 2 is a photo I took on July 11 looking north on the highway showing the skid marks of
19 the pickup and the Kia on the road. I'll mark "P/U" on the photo to identify the pickup's skid marks
20 and "Kia" to identify the other skid, and circle the skid marks. You can see the pedestrian underpass
21 to the left of the road in front of the patrol car.

22   Exhibit 3 is a photo I took from the other side of the road facing south. I'll circle the Kia's skid
23 marks and write "Kia skids" on the photo. The point of impact was right about where the skid marks
24 end. I'll write "Pt. of impact" on the photo and draw an arrow to that point. I'll also draw a circle
25 where Sam came to rest and write that on the photo.

26   Exhibit 4 is another photo I took. I was looking south again, but this time photographing the
27 truck's skid marks from behind where the truck stopped. I'll circle the skid marks and label them
28 "Truck skids." The truck had been moved by that time. The abutment above the pedestrian under-
29 pass is just in front of the patrol car at the right edge of the picture.

30   Exhibit 5 was taken standing next to the pedestrian underpass, primarily just to show the amount
31 of traffic on the road that day. I was facing south.

32   Exhibit 6 is a view of the pedestrian tunnel and the point where Sam stood and started to cross
33 the highway. He ran from the west side to the east side of the highway.

34   Exhibit 7 is my photo of the front of the Kia. I'll circle the two areas of damage I saw. Snyder
35 stated that they were caused by the collision with the child.

36   Exhibit 8 is a photo I took of the dark blue T-shirt Sam was wearing. His shirt and shorts were
37 collected at the hospital and sent to headquarters where I photographed them. I ultimately gave
38 them to Mrs. Scruggs.

39   Exhibit 9 is the photo of the striped grey athletic shorts Sam was wearing. I recognized both
40 Exhibits 8 and 9 from having seen them on the child at the scene.

1   Exhibit 10 is a hand-lettered sign for a softball game. I had heard from one of the witnesses at
2   the scene that Sam had been at the softball field shortly before the accident. I went to that area of
3   the park to see if there were other witnesses there. While in the vicinity of the ball field, I saw this
4   sign and took a picture of it just in case it could be important.
5   Exhibits 11A and 11B are two pictures I took that same day in the park on the east side of
6   the highway. The top picture, 11A, shows the pedestrian tunnel and the sign directing people to
7   it, as well as to the softball field and tennis and basketball courts. I took it just in case somebody
8   wanted to sue the state. You never know. I wanted to show that the underpass is clearly marked.
9   11B is the other side of the same sign.
10   My initial determination was that Snyder was not at fault for the accident, rather that it was
11   caused by the pedestrian failing to yield to traffic. My follow-up investigation the next day seemed
12   to confirm this. However, knowing now that Snyder was on the phone, my opinion that Snyder
13   could not reasonably have avoided the accident is less confident, with both drinking and distraction
14   in the background.

I have read the foregoing deposition and hereby affix my signature that the same is true and correct except as noted herein.

Sandy Fielder

—————————————————
Signature of Deponent

This deposition was taken in the office of plaintiffs' counsel on April 27, *[1 yr ago]*. This deposition was given under oath and was read and signed by the deponent.

Certified by:

Penelope Harrison

—————————————————
Penelope Harrison
Certified Shorthand Reporter
(CSR)

DEPOSITION OF ALEX FLYBERG

July 30, *[1 yr ago]*

1   My name is Alex Flyberg. I am forty-three years old. I live at 1829 Locust Avenue in Nita City.

2   Around 1:00 p.m. on Sunday, July 11, *[2 yrs ago]*, I was driving my black Ford pickup truck, tow-

3   ing my 14-foot aluminum fishing boat on a trailer. I was coming back from a morning of fishing with

4   my good friend, Terry Nettles. That's when the boy got hit by the car.

5   I'm a forklift operator for Wal-Mart. I've worked there for seven years. Before that, I drove a fork-

6   lift for UPS for ten years in a transshipment warehouse. I have a high-school education and served

7   in the U.S. Navy for eight years. I'm divorced with three children who live with my ex-spouse. Terry

8   works with me. We both worked on Saturday that weekend. We got paid overtime.

9   Terry and I got up about 4:00 that morning and headed out for the bay for a morning of fishing.

10   We put in at the bay just north of Bayview State Park around 6:00 a.m. I know a good spot there. We

11   fished all morning and caught a few. Threw all but two or three back. We brought our lunch and a

12   "half-rack" of Bud. You know, a half a case: twelve Buds. We had an ice chest full of bait and Buds.

13   It was a perfect day: clear, sunny, not too hot. We were on the water close on to six hours. We quit

14   around 12:30 p.m. The fish stop biting around mid-day till late afternoon, so there's no use staying

15   out unless you just like to drown worms. Yes, we were tired. The sun kinda saps your energy. Terry

16   was sound asleep in the truck when the accident happened and nearly went through the windshield.

17   Lucky Terry had the seatbelt on. We drank all but a couple of those Buds before and during lunch. But

18   we weren't drunk, more tired than anything. If I had been intoxicated, I would have hit that kid. But

19   I wasn't, and I didn't.

20   The traffic was not too bad. Exhibit 5 is a photo that shows about how the traffic was that day.

21   Cars were driving about five to ten car lengths apart. Though the posted speed is 55 mph, we were

22   going about 45 mph as we headed south on the Sun Coast Highway. It's a two-lane road most of the

23   way, and once you get stuck behind a line of traffic, there is no point in passing. There were just as

24   many cars coming in the other direction as there were in ours. There were several cars in front of me,

25   if I remember right. Regular compact passenger cars. The one directly in front of me was about seven

26   to eight car lengths ahead. I like to keep back from vehicles when I'm towing a trailer. Takes longer for

27   me to stop if there is an emergency. You never can tell when some fool is going to stop to make a left

28   turn without any warning. Also, the park was pretty crowded that weekend.

29   As I was driving near the entrance to the state park, I saw a little boy jog up to the fog line on my

30   side of the road. He came out of a concave grassy area right next to what I later saw was a pedestrian

31   tunnel under the road. I can't imagine why he didn't use it. I saw the boy hesitate at the fog line at

32   the edge of the road for maybe two or three seconds, looking both ways. At point, he was in the

1 sunlight. I knew right then that he was going to try to across the road. It was just a hunch, but I was
2 right. A split second before he took off, I hit the brakes as hard as I could and yelled for Terry to hold
3 on. The whole truck was shuddering and shaking. Smoke was pouring out from the wheel wells. I was
4 sure I was going to hit him, but I didn't. Nearly scared me to death.

5 He was just a blur as he slipped by my left fender, running fast. After that, I lost sight of him
6 until we stopped, and I looked back in my rearview mirror. The cars on the other side of the road
7 were swerving, scattering every which way trying to avoid hitting each other. Terry asked me what
8 happened. I said a boy just ran into the traffic, and I thought he got hit by a car coming in the other
9 direction. I said I didn't think I hit him. When I saw cars pulling off the road, I knew he got hit.

10 I don't recall much about the car that hit the boy. We all stopped and ran to where the boy was ly-
11 ing on the road. We all were asking each other if 911 had been called. The police and state troopers got
12 there quick. The boy was unconscious but alive when I first saw him. He came to later and was taken
13 away by the EMTs. His folks were hysterical, and the driver of the car that hit the boy was saying he/
14 she didn't have enough time to stop. A state trooper asked me what I saw. I noticed that the trooper
15 did some drunk driving tests on the driver but did not arrest him/her.

16 The photo marked Exhibit 2 shows the scene after the boy was taken away. Exhibit 4 shows my
17 skid marks. The boy started across the road about where the patrol car is at the right edge of the pic-
18 ture. Exhibit 5 shows the hill leading up to the ball field to the right and the approximate location of
19 where the boy came up to the road. In the photo labeled Exhibit 6, the car in the picture is just about
20 where my truck was when I hit my brakes. The boy came from the vicinity of the telephone pole.

I have read the foregoing deposition and hereby affix my signature that the same is true and correct
except as noted herein.

Alex Flyberg

—————————————————
Signature of Deponent

This deposition was taken in the office of plaintiffs' counsel on July 30, *[1 yr ago]*. This deposition
was given under oath and was read and signed by the deponent.

Certified by:

Penelope Harrison

—————————————————
Penelope Harrison
Certified Shorthand Reporter
(CSR)

DEPOSITION OF JAN MORIARITY

April 29, *[1 yr ago]*

1   My name is Jan Moriarity. I live at 6016 Town Road, Shell Beach, Nita. My spouse and I retired
2   to an area not far from Bayview State Park and Nita City, where our kids live and work. I am sixty-
3   six years old. Before I retired, I managed a tire store in Nita City. There is a casino in Shell Beach,
4   The Cascade, for which I drive a shuttle bus to and from Nita City. I do it to earn a little extra
5   money and stay busy. I found out that you can't play golf or bridge or hang around the house all
6   day. I have a regular route that I run between the casino and Nita City up and down the Sun Coast
7   Highway. I am very familiar with the highway where it cuts through Bayview State Park. It is almost
8   a two hours' drive one way. I'd been making that run about twice a day, two days a week for about
9   six months before the accident.

10   The shuttle I drive is a nine-passenger van. Sitting in the driver's seat is like being in a pickup
11   or an SUV. I was driving the shuttle on July 11, *[2 yrs ago]*, 1:00 p.m. I remember that day. The car
12   in front of me struck a child who darted across the road in Bayview State Park. I was headed north-
13   bound. Exhibit 2 shows the road as you go north at the point of the accident. I was in a line of cars
14   that was going only about 35–40 mph, very much like the traffic shown in Exhibit 5. Traffic wasn't
15   as heavy as you'd expect at the end of the weekend. It was too early in the day—before folks pack up
16   and head home. We were all going the same speed and were about five car lengths or so apart. The
17   same was true for the traffic in the other direction. That part of the highway is only two lanes and
18   virtually level. It was a clear, sunny, dry day.

19   As I rounded the curve just after the sign for Bayview State Park, I was chatting with one of
20   my passengers—I recall I was trying to explain craps to him. Then, I heard a pickup truck pulling
21   a boat in the oncoming, southbound lane slam on its brakes. I looked and saw smoke coming from
22   its wheels as it was skidding down the road. Then I noticed the boy. He had run past the truck and
23   directly into the path of the car in front of me. That car jammed its brakes and skidded right into
24   the child. It was heart-stopping, terrifying. The child flew in the air, probably 30–40 feet, just like
25   a rag doll.

26   It happened so fast. It was just like: "screech-bang." That fast. It seems like in less than a second
27   it was over. I never saw the kid before the truck hit its brakes. By that time the kid was sprinting
28   directly into the path of the car in front of me. The line of oncoming cars was about the same as my
29   line of traffic. The car in front of the truck could have shielded the boy from our view. I don't know.
30   Who could imagine a kid, even six or seven years old, would do something that stupid? That driver
31   never had a chance to avoid him.

1   Could I see the driver in the car in front of me before the accident? Sure. I was behind the car for
2   several miles—at least fifteen minutes or so. I don't recall seeing the driver talking on a cell phone at
3   any time while I was behind the car. I don't recall whether there was one or two people in the car ahead
4   of me. My seat in the van is a little higher off the road than that of a compact car, and I was talking
5   from time to time with a couple of my passengers, but the car was far enough in front of me—five or
6   so car lengths—that I could see the driver's head and the top of his/her shoulders, or at least the por-
7   tions not obscured by the headrest.

8   I pulled over and hung around till the authorities arrived. Others were caring for the boy. I radioed
9   my dispatcher and told her to call the State Patrol. Later, I went to the trooper who was talking to eye-
10   witnesses and volunteered what I knew. The trooper performed some field sobriety tests on the driver
11   who hit the kid, but did not arrest him/her, so I guess he/she was OK.

I have read the foregoing deposition and hereby affix my signature that the same is true and correct except as noted herein.

Jan Moriarity

_____
Signature of Deponent

This deposition was taken in the office of defendant's counsel on April 29, *[1 yr ago]*. This deposition was given under oath and was read and signed by the deponent.

Certified by:

Merry Fingers

_____
Merry Fingers
Certified Shorthand Reporter
(CSR)

DEPOSITION OF DALE NEWCOMB

August 15, *[1 yr ago]*

1 My name is Dale Newcomb. I am fifty-two years old. I am an accident reconstruction expert.
2 I own my own business, NFG, Newcomb Forensic Graphics. After graduating from Nita Polytech
3 thirty years ago, I was a trooper with the Nita State Patrol. After two years as a regular patrol officer, I
4 worked for twenty years in the major accident investigation section of the Nita State Patrol. I've owned
5 NGF for the last eight years.

6 My business is located in Nita City where I live at 5242 Jennifer Street with my spouse, Cameron.
7 I have one child, Jill, who is a student at Nita Polytech.

8 In college, I took advanced computer science and physics courses. While with the State Patrol ma-
9 jor accident section, I attended two advanced accident reconstruction courses: one at the Northwestern
10 University Traffic Institute fifteen years ago and the other at Texas A&M thirteen years ago. I cur-
11 rently teach a course, part-time, in accident reconstruction at Nita Polytech. It deals with the basics of
12 how a traffic accident is reconstructed and converted into a computer-generated, animated recreation
13 of the accident. The course at Northwestern dealt with advanced accident reconstruction principles,
14 while the A&M course dealt more with computer animation technology.

15 I was asked by plaintiffs' counsel to recreate the auto-pedestrian collision on July 11, *[2 yrs ago]*,
16 involving Sam Scruggs and the car being driven by Lynn Snyder. I was asked by plaintiffs' counsel
17 to do a time and position analysis of the collision and several computer-animated feasibility studies.
18 In preparing these studies, I have reviewed the reports and photos of the Nita State Patrol relating to
19 this accident, as well as the witnesses' depositions. I visited the scene of the accident and checked the
20 measurements done by the troopers. Although my visit was in early February of the year following
21 the accident, the PK spikes the State Patrol drove into the roadbed to mark the beginning and end of
22 all the relevant skid marks were still there, as were the various landmarks that they used as reference
23 points. Finally, I prepared a detailed chart of the accident site showing the skid marks and other rel-
24 evant physical features. That is marked as Exhibit 28. Exhibit 28A is a blowup of part of 28, showing
25 the skid marks more clearly.

26 The Kia's right skid was 64' 11"; the left was 59' 4" according to both my and the State Patrol's
27 measurements. The truck was much heavier and took longer to stop than the Kia, skidding past the
28 reference point until it finally came to a stop. The truck's left tire skidded 126' 6" and its right tire
29 104'8". Determining the length of skid marks like this is a straight measurement, done in relation
30 to the reference point. For greater simplicity, the troopers who came to the scene after the accident
31 condensed the information, taking measurements with west and south coordinates. They laid out a
32 measuring tape along the fog line in the Kia's direction of travel and came up with all of their numbers

NATIONAL INSTITUTE FOR TRIAL ADVOCACY

in relation to both this tape and the reference point. The accident scene was relatively compact and easy to measure, requiring only one tape.

It is not at all unusual for the left and right skid marks for the same car to be different lengths. Though roads feel level to drivers, they are crowned for drainage purposes. The centerline is always the high point. The right tires are lower than the left tires. The downhill tires on the right will nearly always leave marks sooner than their counterparts on the left, closer to the centerline. While there can be other factors at work, such as variations in brake shoe and tire tread wear, the differences in skid marks in this case are most likely a reflection of the road slope. The front tires usually end up being the ones that leave actual skid marks, which are melted tar, not rubber, on asphalt roadways. This is because of the dramatic weight shift to the front of the car in emergency braking, putting far more pressure on the front wheels. The rear wheels often track over the front wheels in this process.

As a preliminary matter, I needed to establish a speed for the child and for the striking vehicle, a new Kia with less than ten thousand miles on it. My calculation of the vehicle's speed was based on the skid marks laid down by the car. A coefficient of friction, which is determined by the computer based upon the data we input regarding the condition of the road and tires and the weight of the vehicle, is applied to the skid measurement to determine the speed the car was traveling when the brakes were hit and the rate it slowed while skidding. I used the figure 0.7 g's. Because the road surface was uniform, I assumed the car slowed at a constant rate. Taking into account the length of the car's skid marks and the coefficient of friction, the computer determined that the speed of the Kia prior to braking was approximately 35 mph. This is corroborated by the statements of the witnesses and the defendant, who put the speed of the traffic in the defendant's line of traffic at about 35–40 mph. I chose to use the more conservative speed to give the defendant the benefit of the doubt.

As for the boy's speed, the witnesses said he took off running at full speed from the edge of the road and was running when hit. There was no wide variation on where the boy was when he started to run. As an accident reconstructionist, I am familiar with published data regarding the running speed of children. I learned that the boy was a slim, normal six-year-old. While there is a range of top speeds that young boys can run, I assigned a speed at the fiftieth percentile, which is 7.5 mph or around 11.2 feet per second, in order to make him neither slower nor faster than the average boy at that age. At this rate, it would have taken him three seconds to run, without hesitating, from the fog line at the left shoulder of the road to the point of impact near the right shoulder, which was about 34 feet. I also assumed that the boy reached his top speed almost immediately. This is generally true of children, who are able to start fast and maintain that speed for short bursts.

One witness said the boy hesitated at the center of the roadway. I did not factor this into the boy's speed or any of my other calculations. It would have been too arbitrary to pick a length of time for the hesitation. I thought it better to take a conservative figure here that would give the driver of the Kia the benefit of the doubt. Of course, if the child did hesitate at the centerline, then the boy would have taken longer to get to the point of impact and the driver would have had more time to see and avoid him.

I also factored into my calculations that the boy's path was straight across the highway. If I had used a diagonal path away from the defendant's car, this too would have given the driver even more time to react and avoid the child. I did not do this, as I wanted to give the Kia driver the benefit of the doubt.

1   I estimated the point of impact between the car and boy by applying basic principles of physics re-
2 garding the transfer of energy. I used the speed of the car when it hit the boy (about 20 mph as it was
3 braking), the boy's weight, where he landed, the dent on the Kia's front bumper and hood, and the loca-
4 tion of the boy's tennis shoe to calculate how far the boy was thrown and, thus, where the front of the car
5 was at impact. I also relied on the statements of the witnesses, as to where the boy was at the side of the
6 road, to corroborate my determination, assuming, as I did, that he ran straight across the road.

7   An accident reconstructionist must have insight into common driving strategies and tactics. Realisti-
8 cally, when this child stepped to the fog line he became a potential hazard for motorists to take note of.
9 We all know that children are impulsive, particularly younger children. Accordingly, an alert and respon-
10 sible driver would have anticipated a potential emergency stop at this point. A fidgeting kid at the edge of
11 the road (or as one witness described him, one who looked like he was taking a runner's stance preparing
12 to sprint across the road) is a sure sign of trouble. A responsible driver, seeing this, would at least take
13 his foot off the gas and cover or touch the brake pedal, ready to stop quicker if necessary. Snyder stated
14 in his/her deposition that he/she did not take his/her foot off the gas when the child was noticed by the
15 road. This caused Snyder's reaction time to be a fraction of a second longer than it would have been if the
16 driver was covering the brake pedal at that point. The computer calculations demonstrate that Snyder's
17 failure to do that was the difference between hitting and not hitting the child.

18   I do not see this as a classic "child dart out" case because the driver of the Kia had a couple of warn-
19 ings before the child started into the road. First, the driver noticed the boy by the road. In the classic "dart
20 out" case, the child runs out from between parked cars without being seen first. Second, the truck in the
21 southbound lane, closest to where the child was standing, slammed on its brakes first, creating smoke and
22 screeching tire noise. These were both visual and auditory warnings to the Kia driver, which if he/she had
23 noticed and reacted to, would have allowed the child to run past the Kia unharmed.

24   That the southbound truck missed the boy illustrates how poorly the Kia driver reacted to the obvi-
25 ous danger. Taking into account the 45 mph speed of the truck and the distance it would travel during
26 an assumed 1.5 second reaction time for the driver (who was older and had been drinking steadily that
27 day), I determined that the truck was about 215 feet from the boy when the driver spotted the danger and
28 began to brake. It traveled 121 feet before it began to skid. I estimate the truck was about 94 feet from the
29 boy's path when it began skidding. It was much heavier, particularly when pulling a loaded boat trailer. It
30 took twice as much distance for the truck to come to a stop than the Kia. The Kia was over 140 feet away
31 from the point of impact when the child started his dash across the road. The driver of the southbound
32 truck had much less time to react than the Kia driver. The boy's dash was less foreseeable for the truck
33 driver than for the Kia driver because the Kia had the truck braking noise and smoke as additional warn-
34 ing. If any vehicle should have hit the child, it was the truck. Yet, it avoided the accident.

35   Also, the witnesses testified that the traffic was not bumper-to-bumper, that there were five to ten
36 car spaces between the vehicles on both sides of the road. Therefore, there couldn't have been a vehicle in
37 front of the truck close enough to obscure the vision of the oncoming Kia. Also, a vehicle in front of the
38 southbound truck would have blocked the Kia's view of the child for only a fraction of a second.

39   Based upon all the data, I prepared some computer animations. Each runs twice on the video. The
40 first animation is a recreation of how the collision actually happened from the perspective of the driver

1   of the Kia. This shows the collision at real-time speed, meaning this is actually how fast it all happened

2   and what could be seen from Snyder's vantage point. In these video simulations, we have added a red

3   light just beneath the windshield to indicate when, according to my computer calculations, Snyder

4   applied the brakes.

5   According to my calculations, Sam would have been about 275 feet from the Kia when he became

6   visible to the Kia driver, assuming Sam was at the side of the road then. However, I assumed that the

7   Kia driver may not have either seen or realized that there was a child by the road, or appreciated that

8   the child might try to cross the road at that point in time. Thus, in figuring how much time the Kia

9   driver had to react before the collision with the child, I did not start the clock, so to speak, until the

10 car was about 200 feet from the point of impact and from roughly where the boy was by the side of

11 the road.

12   The first simulation shows how visible Sam was at the side of the road when the Kia was approxi-

13 mately 200 feet from the point of impact. At the point when the boy began his run into the road, the

14 Kia driver had about three seconds to see the boy, appreciate the danger, and begin braking. If the

15 driver had begun braking at that time, the boy clearly would not have been hit. About one second of

16 this three-second window was taken up with the car skidding 65 feet. That leaves about two seconds to

17 react and begin braking from the point at which the child could be clearly seen starting his run from

18 the side of the road 200 feet away.

19   The first animation also shows what the Kia driver would see when the truck hit its brakes and

20 began to skid, just missing the boy. At this point, the Kia would be about 90 feet from impact point.

21 Even if the Kia driver had delayed braking until this point in time, there would have been no collision

22 with the boy. My third animation, Feasibility Study #2, demonstrates this.

23   But, as the first animation shows, the Kia did not begin to brake and skid until Sam just crossed

24 the centerline of the road. When the red brake indicator light goes on, the Kia was only about 40 feet

25 from impact and laid down 65 feet of skid marks. By that time, it was too late to avoid hitting the boy

26 as shown in the video. In all of the animations, I assumed that Snyder was going 35 mph when he/she

27 began to brake. If Snyder had been going faster, it would have taken longer to stop, obviously, but I

28 picked a conservative speed favorable to Snyder.

29   Even as late as the Kia braked, the child nearly cleared the path of the Kia. If he had been able to

30 run another 3.5 feet, the car would have missed him. This means that if Snyder had braked one-third

31 of a second sooner, there would have been no accident. The Kia did not have to come to a complete

32 stop to avoid the accident. Just getting on the brakes 0.3 seconds sooner would have allowed the child

33 to clear the car.

34   Put another way, according to my computer calculations, if the Kia had begun braking when the

35 car was 53 feet or more from the child, it would have missed him. This distance is illustrated by the

36 photo marked Exhibit 34. After doing my calculations, I revisited the scene and had my assistant stand

37 53 feet from my car. I took that picture.

38   I had stills prepared from the first animation study that show the potential visibility of the child by

39 the roadside to the Kia driver at 275, 200, 90, and 40 feet away from the point of impact. They have

40 been marked Exhibits 29 through 33, respectively.

The second animation, Feasibility Study #1, is a "what if" version of the accident. This animation, based upon all of the data, clearly shows that the car would have been able to avoid hitting the child by a fairly wide margin if the Kia driver had begun to brake as soon as the truck began its panic stop.

The third animation, Feasibility Study #2, was prepared to show what would happen if the Kia driver had begun braking at the point when the truck was well into its skid and the child had just slipped by the left front fender of the truck. Study #2 shows that at this point, when the child is just short of the center line, if the Kia driver had hit the brakes, the Kia would have stopped in time to avoid hitting the child, all other things being constant. At this point, the Kia driver would hear the screeching truck tires, see the smoke from the skidding tires, and have no obstacles between him/her and the child who was almost on the center line. However, the driver apparently still did not notice what was going on in front of him/her.

I did not put any vehicles other than the oncoming truck in the animations as it would be speculative as to where they were positioned at any point in time. Also, I could not be sure what kind of vehicles they were: campers, SUVs, or sedans, for instance. In any event, all the witnesses described the traffic at the time of the accident as being similar to the traffic depicted in Exhibit 5. Given the distances between the vehicles shown there, I concluded that putting oncoming vehicles in the animations was not necessary for them to be fair depictions of what Snyder did and could have seen and done.

Because the accident occurred at 1:00 p.m. Daylight Savings Time in July, the sun would have been directly over head. Therefore, in my animations I eliminated most shadows. It is also true that the boy, Sam, had a dark blue T-shirt on. The animation has the boy dressed as described by the witnesses, a blue T-shirt and light gray shorts showing white legs, arms, and face.

Finally, the feasibility animations show that the boy would not have been hit if the Kia driver had begun to brake any time after the boy left the side of the road up to when he reached the center line. The panic stop by the truck alone should have drawn the attention of the Kia driver to the emergency. And at that point the boy was clearly visible. I have seen the stop-action photos taken the day following the accident by Trooper Fielder. They do not change or affect my opinions in any way. I note that the child in the photos is standing further back from the road than as described by the witnesses. This made the child harder to see in the shadows.

In all of my animations, I assume that the Kia driver's reaction time was one-half a second less than the normal range of three-quarters to one and a half seconds. I did this for two reasons. Studies show that younger drivers have a normal reaction time of about 0.5 seconds if a hazard is anticipated. Snyder meets this profile. Flyberg, the truck driver does not. Secondly, Snyder said he/she saw the boy at the side of the road. Thus, Snyder should have anticipated a possible hazard. When a person does not see and anticipate the hazard, the person spends more reaction time first focusing on and recognizing what he sees, and then realizing that they might need to react to the emergency. But when the person sees and recognizes the cause of the possible emergency before the emergency actually occurs, the reaction time is shorter because much of the mental processing of the perceptions has already occurred. I'm aware of Dr. Louis Charles' book, *Accident Reconstruction Principles*. It is widely regarded as authoritative. However, like all experts, he can be a little dogmatic. Also, I doubt he'd disagree with me about Snyder in these circumstances for the reasons I've given.

1   If Snyder had reacted as a reasonably careful driver would have, that is, took his/her foot off the gas
2   pedal and applied the brake in 0.5 seconds, then we can calculate, based upon the car's skid marks and
3   speed of the car, that Snyder would not have hit the boy. The fact that the car hit the boy shows that
4   Snyder waited too long to brake the car. This would cause one to conclude that the Kia driver must
5   have been distracted or had reaction time impaired by something—to wait that long to begin braking
6   is otherwise difficult to explain.

7   Trooper Fielder's report and Snyder's deposition testimony indicate that Snyder had been drinking
8   margaritas during lunch. More than two, in fact. This was less than two hours before the collision.
9   Although Fielder said Snyder "blew" only a .07, under the legal limit of .08, this could account for
10   Snyder's slow reactions.

11   Moreover, Snyder admits to having been on a cell phone at the time the boy ran into the road.
12   This, too, could have had a significant impact on Snyder's reaction time. Studies have shown that driv-
13   ers are many times more likely to have an accident when they are on the phone than drivers who are
14   not. A national survey estimated that 8 percent of all drivers are on the phone during daylight hours. A
15   2006 University of Utah study indicated that drivers who talk on hand-held or hands-free phones are
16   as impaired as drunk drivers. And a 1997 Canadian study determined that a driver is four times more
17   likely to get into a crash while talking on a cell phone.

18   In short, if Snyder had been fully alert and reacted in the time that he/she could have reacted
19   instead of delaying his/her braking—reacting just 0.3 seconds or more quicker—the boy would have
20   not been hit. I see no other reasons to explain Snyder's slow reaction other than being distracted on the
21   phone or by drinking or both.

22   It is true that outcomes in accident reconstruction depend upon the assumptions you make. If you
23   change the assumptions, you will change the outcomes—by a lot or a little, depending on the par-
24   ticular assumption and how much you change it. Some changes don't have an effect on the ultimate
25   conclusion.

26   I billed my time on this project at $150 per hour and that of my assistant at $75 per hour for such
27   things as phone calls, travel, inspecting Snyder's car, speed analysis, research, report preparation, con-
28   ferences, preparation for this deposition, and testifying today and at trial. My computer simulation
29   work was billed at $200 per hour. At this point, I have billed Sam Scruggs' lawyer around $17,000. If
30   this case goes to trial, I expect to bill about $18,000 total.

I have read the foregoing deposition and hereby affix my signature that the same is true and correct except as noted herein.

Dale Newcomb

——————————————————————
Signature of Deponent

This deposition was taken in the office of defendant's counsel on August 15, *[1 yr ago]*. This deposition was given under oath and was read and signed by the deponent.

Certified by:

Penelope Harrison

Penelope Harrison
Certified Shorthand Reporter
(CSR)

DEPOSITION OF PAT/TAMMY SCRUGGS

June 1, *[1 yr ago]*

1   My name is Pat/Tammy Scruggs. I live at 2227 Flagler Road in Matlock, Nita. I am forty-eight
2   years old and never had my deposition taken before. I have been married to my *[wife Tammy]/[husband*
3   *Pat]* for seventeen years. We have two children, Robin who is sixteen, and Sam who is seven. I have an
4   Associate's degree from Nita Community College in Olympia.

5   [*When the witness is Mrs. Scruggs*: I was a secretary in the office of a mobile home dealership for a
6   few years. That's where I met Pat, who was a salesman there. Now I am an office assistant at the Home
7   Loan Bank in Shelton.]

8   [*When witness is Mr. Scruggs*: I have shifted around in various careers. I was a mobile home sales-
9   man for four or five years. That's where I met Tammy. She was a secretary in the office of the dealer-
10   ship. The last five or six years I have been working in heating, ventilation, and air conditioning in
11   Shelton. I'm a salesman.]

12   We live in the Ever Green Trailer Park in a double-wide mobile home. The area is very rural. The
13   kids are bussed to school every day. We like it. It is nice and quiet and uncrowded.

14   Our favorite form of family recreation is camping. We have an old Winnebago motor home left
15   over from our days in that business. We pile into it and go to some nice part of the state on holidays or
16   just anytime when the weather seems good and the kids are out of school. We even pull our kids out of
17   school sometimes when the weather is particularly good. All of us like the excitement of going to new
18   places and being in the great outdoors and fresh air.

19   We had never been to Bayview State Park before, and since I had to work the Fourth of July week-
20   end last year, we decided to camp there the following weekend. We drove there on Thursday evening,
21   July 8, and were going to leave Monday morning, July 12. We parked our motor home, leveled it, and
22   hooked up to the utilities. On July 9, we took our kids over to the ball field, which is on the other side
23   of the Sun Coast Highway from where we camped. This park is a little unusual in that the highway
24   divides it in two. There is a pedestrian tunnel that goes underneath the road. There are signs pointing
25   it out, as shown in Exhibit 11. I told our kids, several times, to always use the tunnel. Exhibit 1 is an
26   aerial view of that part of the park, showing the tunnel and the ball field. The camp ground is at the
27   bottom of the picture.

28   I have been shown the video of our counsel's "walk through" of the park. It quite accurately
29   shows how you drive into the park; how we drove to our assigned camp site; how one walks from our
30   campsite to the ball field. It shows the sign post pointing to the underpass and the ball field. Then the
31   video goes through the underpass—that's just what it looks like, but it is damp and smelly too—and
32   up the steps to the ball field. Then, the camera shows the trail down the hill from the field that Sam

1   must have taken to not be seen by Robin or the ranger. Then it takes you to the side of the road beside
2   the underpass where Sam stopped before he ran into the road. Finally, the video shows what the road
3   looks like in both directions and then crosses the road at that point. I can't look at it without my blood
4   running cold and feeling a little sick to my stomach, knowing this is where Sam was hit. The video is
5   entirely accurate.

6   Later on July 9, we went to the beach and dug clams. We socialized with another family from our
7   trailer park that was there. Our kids brought their bikes and rode them around the camp grounds
8   meeting other kids and making friends. They were told to always stay within shouting distance of our
9   campsite in case we needed them, like at supper time. In the evenings we played board and card games
10 at our campsite.

11   On July 10, I went off to play golf at a local course. My spouse stayed behind with the kids and
12 went to the beach. Sam was a little bored at times and spent most of the day riding his bike around
13 the campground.

14   During the entire time we were at the park, from July 8 to July 11, none of us ever crossed over the
15 surface of the highway to get to or from the ball field and courts over there, except for when Sam got
16 hit by the car. We always used the tunnel. Exhibits 13 and 16 show the tunnel.

17   On the day Sam was hit, Sunday, July 11, the park ranger posted signs that there was going to be
18 a softball game that afternoon at 1:00. Exhibit 10 looks like one of those signs. Sam wanted to play. I
19 told him that he could go only if there was adult supervision of the game and Robin would take him.
20 I spoke with the park ranger, who said that she would be there supervising the game. That was a first
21 step, but we still needed Sam to get safely there and back.

22   I talked with Robin and his/her new friend, Jessica, who said they planned to play ball that eve-
23 ning. I asked Robin if he/she would take Sam at 1:00 and watch out for him, and he/she agreed. I don't
24 recall reminding him/her or Sam to use the tunnel. I just assumed they would, since we had used it
25 every time we had crossed the road, and I had warned them before several times.

26   I had no reservations about sending Sam off with Robin across the road. Robin is an exceptionally
27 bright and responsible teen who does well in school and loves sports. Our neighbors have been us-
28 ing Robin as a baby-sitter since he/she was thirteen. Robin sits for them all the time and makes good
29 money at it. Our neighbors love and trust Robin.

30   About a half an hour after the kids left our camper, my spouse and I heard the squeal of tires com-
31 ing from the road. We looked at each other, alarmed, and immediately took off running toward the
32 road. There were cars stopped all over the road, and a small crowd of people gathered up the road on the
33 other side. We went there and immediately recognized that the boy lying on the ground was Sam. He
34 was unconscious. Someone said his legs were probably broken. He was scraped up pretty bad. We were
35 in complete panic. Robin was there and said Sam left the field without telling him/her. Robin didn't
36 know why and was terribly upset and crying, as were we. We were told the ambulance had been called.

37   Several State Patrol officers arrived and took control. It seemed forever before the ambulance ar-
38 rived. By that time Sam was awake but crying in pain. I was so relieved to see his eyes open. He was
39 alive! Exhibits 2 and 4 show the scene of the accident after Sam was taken away. Exhibits 8 and 9 look
40 like the T-shirt and shorts Sam was wearing that day.

1   Sam was taken to a hospital in Shell Beach. Before we hastily packed up and headed for Shell
2   Beach to be with Sam, I met the driver of the car that hit Sam. The driver was pretty upset. I didn't
3   know how it happened, so I didn't say anything. The driver came over and said how sorry he/she was,
4   that he/she tried to stop but couldn't in time. The driver's friend kept chattering on about how Sam
5   had run into the road and that how hitting him was unavoidable. I didn't say anything. I was too wor-
6   ried about Sam.

7   Sam can't remember much of that day at all and nothing from an hour or so before he was hit until
8   he was in the hospital. He was a typical six-year-old. He was well behaved; never got into trouble. He
9   generally obeyed our instructions. Sure, like all kids, sometimes we'd have to tell him not to do some-
10   thing more than once. But we trained him to never cross a road without an adult, to look both ways,
11   and to hold the hand of the person with him.

12   Sam has recovered from his two broken legs, but we did not let him play any sports since the ac-
13   cident. Exhibit 21 is a picture I took of Sam's leg brace and cast at the hospital. He had them on for
14   many weeks. He is eating and sleeping okay now and is generally healthy except for the usual problems
15   like ear infections. However, he received a serious concussion, and we, his parents, and his teachers
16   think that he still is not quite right because of the accident. Even though the headaches and fatigue
17   he had for several months are gone now, he is afraid of some things he was not afraid of before. Like
18   water. He loved going on boats. Now, he is quite reluctant to do so. Or to swim. Very strange. And he
19   is very afraid of crossing a road. Also, he sometimes complains of blurry vision, especially when looking
20   at distances, like at the blackboard at school.

21   However, our major concern is about his learning and attention. Ever since the accident, he seems
22   slightly, well, "spaced out." I don't know how to describe it. It is harder to get his attention, and he
23   seems more impulsive. You sometimes have to tell him something more than once before he under-
24   stands. Since the accident, his grades have been poor in first grade, and his teachers think he's changed
25   from how he was in kindergarten. They say he acts like he has that attention deficit problem—ADD
26   or ADHD—whatever. Dr. Zindell was afraid of this and sent Sam to Dr. McClaren for tests. Dr. Mc-
27   Claren told us that the tests show Sam is suffering from a brain impairment that makes it harder for
28   him to understand words and to be easily distracted. We are thinking about having him try a medicine
29   for ADD, but haven't done that yet.

30   We are afraid that Sam will fall behind in school and need special tutoring. Dr. McClaren has
31   recommended some tutoring and special accommodations for Sam at school. This is all consistent with
32   Sam's behavior after the accident that we have observed. We are fearful that Sam is now permanently
33   "developmentally challenged" or whatever the proper name is for it.

I have read the foregoing deposition and hereby affix my signature that the same is true and correct
except as noted herein.

_____
Signature of Deponent

This deposition was taken in the office of plaintiffs' attorney on June 1, *[1 yr ago]*. This deposition was given under oath and was read and signed by the deponent.

Certified by:

Penelope Harrison
Certified Shorthand Reporter
(CSR)

DEPOSITION OF ROBIN SCRUGGS

August 2, *[1 yr ago]*

1   My name is Robin Scruggs. I am sixteen years old. I live with my family at 2227 Flagler Road in

2   Matlock, Nita, in the Ever Green Trailer Park. I was fifteen when my brother, Sam, was hit by the car.

3   Sam was six years old then. I am about to enter Cedar Park High School in the tenth grade. I enjoy

4   school and got good grades at Cedar Park Middle School, mostly A's. I played softball and soccer. I'm

5   going to go out for lacrosse in high school. I want to be a goalie.

6   I like children and regularly make extra money by baby-sitting for neighbors, with a job every

7   weekend or two. I make $3.50 an hour. I've taken care of kids as young as three. I've been baby-sitting

8   since I was thirteen, after I took a class in child care at Children's Hospital.

9   My family loves to camp. The weekend after the long Fourth of July weekend last year, my father,

10   mother, brother, and I went camping at Bayview State Park. We had never been there before. We got

11   there the evening of Thursday, July 8 and pitched tents for me and Sam. Mom and dad slept in our old

12   Winnebago motor home. The park baseball field and tennis courts are across the Sun Coast Highway

13   from the camping area. There is a tunnel under the highway so people don't have to try to cross the

14   road, which was pretty busy all the time.

15   The two pictures you are showing me with "Exhibit 11" on them is a picture of the park signs

16   in the campground pointing you to the underpass and the ball field. Sam and I went with my father

17   through the tunnel to check out that part of the park. Dad told me and Sam that we should always use

18   the tunnel. Sam and I went there, through the tunnel, on Saturday too. The diagram you are showing

19   me of the roadway looks accurate. It is marked Exhibit 28.

20   I have seen our lawyer's video recording of a walk through the park. It shows just what it looks like

21   from the time you enter the park, drive to our campsite that weekend, and what it looks like when you

22   walk from our camp to the ball field under the highway. It shows the tree where Sam was sitting and

23   the path down the hill from the field to the road that Sam must have taken to not be seen by me. Also

24   it shows what the highway looks like both ways at the point where Sam was hit.

25   On Sunday afternoon, the day Sam was hit, he wanted to go to the ball field to play softball. We

26   had seen a sign in the campgrounds saying that there would be a softball game for kids Sam's age at

27   1:00 p.m. The exhibit with number 10 on it looks like that sign. Mom asked if I would take Sam to

28   the field and watch him. Since I just wanted to hang around and get to know my new friend Jessica,

29   who I met at the park that weekend, Jessica and I agreed to take Sam to the game and hang out there.

30   Also, I knew that they might let older kids play if they didn't have enough for two sides, and both Jes-

31   sica and I wanted to play, so I had no problem with this. My parents knew the park ranger would be

32   there supervising the game.

1   The three of us used the tunnel to walk to the ball field. The tunnel is dark, damp, and kinda
2   smelly. We ran through it as quickly as we could. I don't recall what Sam was wearing other than a T-
3   shirt and shorts. The photo marked Exhibit 1 looks like a photo from an airplane of the park. It shows
4   the road, the ball field, the tennis courts, and the underpass. Exhibit 6 is a picture of the underpass.

5   When we got to the ball field, the ranger was there with a bag of bats and balls. There were some
6   younger kids running around the field, but no game was going on yet. The ranger dumped the bats
7   and balls out and told us he would help organize us into teams. As I suspected would be the case, there
8   were not enough younger kids to form two teams, so the ranger said everyone could play. Sam said
9   it wasn't fair for the older kids to play and said he wouldn't play. I tried to get Sam to join in, but he
10 refused. I told him to stay in the area, where I could keep an eye on him while the rest of us played.
11 Sam usually minds me. He went over to a tree behind the backstop and started bouncing up and down
12 on a limb, sulking, I guess. I told him to stay there.

13 The ranger was acting as the umpire, standing behind the pitcher. I was playing catcher. It could
14 not have been more than a few minutes later when I heard screeching of car tires. I turned and saw Sam
15 was nowhere in sight. I called for him. When I got no answer, I suddenly got that hollow feeling in the
16 pit of my stomach. I knew something bad had happened. I ran to the edge of the hill leading down to
17 the highway and the tunnel. On the other side of the road, there was Sam lying on the shoulder. Cars
18 were all stopped and scattered about. I ran to him and told a man and woman there that he was my
19 brother. The woman told me to go get my parents quick.

20 I ran to our camp site to get mom and dad but they were already on the way. When I told them it
21 was Sam, they said, "Oh, my God!" and ran with me to the highway. Sam was awake, rolling in pain.
22 The ambulance took him to the hospital a little later. The people there were saying that Sam tried to
23 run across the road and was hit. I can't understand why he'd do that. Maybe he was afraid of the tun-
24 nel. He told me later that he could not remember anything that happened that day after lunch until he
25 was in the ambulance on the way to the hospital.

26 Sam is usually very obedient and responsible. It never entered my mind that he'd go off on his
27 own like that. It was very unlike him. I remember looking over a few times and seeing him on the tree
28 limb prior to hearing the tire screech. I don't know when he left the tree, but it couldn't have been long
29 before.

30 The accident broke both Sam's legs and hurt his head. He was often in pain when he was in the
31 casts. His rehabilitation was not easy. He also complained a lot of headaches for months after the ac-
32 cident. Those have gone away it seems, and Sam is back to running around. His legs seem fine, thank
33 goodness.

34 Ever since the accident, Sam has been a little different. He seems kinda, well, I hate to say this, but
35 he doesn't seem quite as quick as he was before the accident. It is hard to give you an example. He just
36 seems to need things to be explained to him a couple of times for him to get it. That wasn't true before.
37 He was quick. And I think he's not doing as well in school as before.

I have read the foregoing deposition and hereby affix my signature that the same is true and correct except as noted herein.

Robin Scruggs

Signature of Deponent

This deposition was taken in the office of defendant's counsel on August 2, *[1 yr ago]*. This deposition was given under oath and was read and signed by the deponent.

Certified by:

Tran Stanscript

Tran Stanscript
Certified Shorthand Reporter
(CSR)

DEPOSITION OF LYNN SNYDER

July 12, *[1 yr ago]*

[Note: it is to be assumed that Divindra Patel is the same gender as Lynn Snyder.]

1   My name is Lynn Snyder. I am twenty-eight years old. I currently live at 220 Maple Street,
2   Brookline, Massachusetts. I am a postdoctoral researcher in the Department of Computer Science at
3   Massachusetts Institute of Technology. I am single and share an apartment with an MIT student. I was
4   raised in Philadelphia, Pennsylvania.

5   Last year, in the spring of *[2 yrs ago]*, a classmate of mine from my undergraduate days, Divindra
6   Patel, was working on his/her PhD in electrical engineering at the University of Nita. He/she was a
7   visiting foreign student from India. We had not seen each other for over a year. I called Divindra and
8   suggested we take a vacation from our studies. Divindra suggested that I fly out to Nita and that we
9   spend a few days in the Shell Beach area of Nita, which he/she described as very beautiful. It is about a
10   two hour drive from Nita City where Divindra lived. I agreed and flew out to Nita City on Wednesday,
11   the seventh of July. I stayed at Divindra's apartment that night. Then, on Thursday, July 8, we rented
12   a car and drove to Shell Beach, where we stayed in an inexpensive motel. July 8, 9, and 10 we did some
13   fishing, hiking, playing the Shell Beach Casino slots, and generally relaxed and ate a lot of seafood. We
14   did not visit Bayview State Park.

15   To save money, I rented the cheapest car I could, a new Kia sedan. I have an old Toyota Tercel in
16   Brookline, but I don't drive it much, mainly on weekends. I rely on public transportation mostly. The
17   exhibit you are showing me, number 7, is a picture of the rented Kia. I remember the dents and the
18   license number.

19   The drive from Nita City to Shell Beach took us up the Sun Coast Highway through Bayview
20   State Park, past the very spot where I had the accident with the Scruggs boy a few days later. Traffic
21   was light. I drove at all times, since I rented it and did not want to pay the extra insurance coverage if
22   Divindra drove. As we drove through the Park on the way to Shell Beach, I did see a pedestrian or two
23   along the road and maybe one crossing the road on foot.

24   On Sunday, July 11, after treating ourselves to a large seafood brunch, we packed up and started
25   our drive back to Nita City about 12:30 p.m. We expected to reach the Nita City airport about 2:30
26   p.m. I had a 3:30 p.m. flight to Chicago, connecting to Boston. I was going to get to Boston around
27   dinner time. I had to be at school the next morning for a meeting with my supervisor.

28   There was pretty consistent traffic on the Sun Coast Highway, but it wasn't real heavy bumper-
29   to-bumper. The Fourth of July weekend was the previous weekend so there weren't a lot of campers
30   generally, and it was too early in the day for the weekend vacationers to be heading home. Looking at
31   Exhibit 5, a photo taken not too long after the accident, I believe, it pretty accurately shows how the
32   traffic was through the park. I think there were five to eight car lengths separating me and the vehicles

1   in front and behind me. We reached Bayview Park around 1:00 p.m. I was driving. It was still sunny,
2   dry, and clear—a beautiful day.

3   Although the speed limit on the highway at that point is 55 mph, the line of traffic I was in was
4   going only about 35 to 45 mph. I was a little concerned whether I'd make my flight if the traffic was
5   this slow all the way to Nita City, but, still, I had lots of time and assumed things would speed up once
6   we got past the two-lane stretch of the road through the park. Before we reached the park, I may have
7   passed a few poky cars when the opportunity arose, but I wasn't in a hurry yet.

8   While still in the park, I rounded a curve and came to a straightaway. There was a sign that said
9   the park entrance was ahead, but it had no further information or warnings. I was still about five car
10 lengths behind a small pickup truck, and a shuttle van was several car lengths behind me. There was
11 also a steady line of vehicles headed south in the opposite direction, all roughly five or so car lengths
12 apart.

13   While on this straightaway approaching the park entrance, I saw a small boy standing on the
14 shoulder on the opposite side of the road to my left ahead of me. I really can't estimate how far ahead
15 of me he was. I'm bad at distances, and I was moving at about 35–40 mph in his direction. Maybe he
16 was almost a half a football field's distance ahead of me—one hundred and fifty feet or so—when I
17 first noticed him. Maybe less. I did not take my foot off the gas. I realize that children are impulsive
18 and unpredictable, but I had no reason to suspect that the child would dart into the road. With the
19 traffic, he could not cross safely. There was no crosswalk there, no traffic light. The boy was just stand-
20 ing there, like he was waiting for someone to pick him up. So, I had no reason not to just keep moving
21 with the rest of the traffic. None of the vehicles ahead of me in my lane or the opposite lane put on
22 their brakes.

23   Shortly after first noticing the boy, he made a few steps toward the road but then stopped at the
24 edge of the road at the fog line. I kept my foot on the gas pedal in order to keep up with the flow of
25 the traffic in my lane and was looking ahead. I didn't notice the child again until after he made a run
26 for it, and the traffic in the oncoming lane began to slam on their brakes. I recall a pickup pulling a
27 boat in the oncoming lane braking hard: smoking tires, the screech of brakes. Then, I saw him to my
28 left in the road and slammed on my brakes as hard as I could. I thought the boy had been hit by the
29 oncoming truck. Divindra would have gone through the windshield but for the seatbelt. The truck
30 missed the boy, but he continued, running into my lane. Unfortunately, I skidded into the boy and hit
31 his legs on the passenger side of my car. He flew in the air, hit my windshield, and fell on the ground
32 ahead of me. I immediately pulled over and ran to him, saying, "Oh, my God! Why did you do that!"
33 My friend also ran over. The boy, who was six or seven years old, was not conscious at that point. Cars
34 stopped and people began to gather around. I told them I couldn't avoid him. Some of the other drivers
35 remarked on how foolish the boy had been and consoled me, saying that it wasn't my fault. Someone
36 called 911. Soon the state police and an ambulance arrived.

37   I was in complete shock. I don't remember much. I was at the scene for at least an hour. I remember
38 seeing the boy's parents there. They were understandably distraught. I tried to tell them that it was not
39 my fault, that I tried to stop but he ran right in front of me. I couldn't avoid him. I told them that I
40 hoped he would be okay.

1   When I was speaking to a trooper, he/she said me and Divindra smelled like alcohol. Asked if I had
2   been drinking, I admitted to having a couple margaritas during brunch and maybe one before brunch.
3   I felt totally fine. We had a large brunch and only a few drinks. Trooper Fielder, I think was the name,
4   said that he/she was required to give me some field sobriety tests, so we walked down the highway a
5   short distance. First, Fielder required me to walk heel-to-toe along the fog line of the highway. (Traffic
6   was being routed into the middle lane at that point.) I did fine. Then, the trooper had me stand with
7   my feet together, arms outstretched to the side, eyes closed, head tilted all the way back, and touch my
8   nose with my index fingers several times. I had no problems. Finally, the trooper asked me to count
9   backwards from seventy-three to sixty-one, which I could do. Then the officer had me blow into a
10   portable field breathalyzer or something. After blowing in it, Fielder said, ".07. You're OK, just barely.
11   I'm not going to hold you for drunk driving." The trooper seemed quite sympathetic towards me. I was
12   not given a ticket or anything. Eventually, they said I could go.

13   Divindra and I had been having a conversation about our travel plans in the minutes prior to the
14   impact. I now recall that I was on my cell phone talking with the airline to find out if the 3:30 flight
15   I booked was the last flight of the day or if there was a later flight. I had dialed the airline information
16   number and given Divindra my return ticket. I may have been talking to the ticket agent when the
17   accident happened. Yes, I did tell the trooper that I was not on the phone when the accident occurred.
18   I was in shock. I panicked and lied. I shouldn't have. It was a stupid thing to do since it made no dif-
19   ference at all.

20   Ultimately, I did miss my flight. I stayed with Divindra that evening and caught a flight the next
21   day. I missed my meeting with my supervisor. She left the country that afternoon, but it wasn't that
22   important. We were to go over the results of my latest research. I met with her the following month
23   after she got back from her trip to China. No, she is no longer my supervisor. I now have another. She
24   said she was not satisfied with my research, but my current supervisor is.

25   Exhibit 2 is a photograph of the accident scene sometime after the boy was taken away. You can
26   see my car off the side of the road. The camera is facing north, the direction I was headed, but it is on
27   the side of the road where the kid came from. Exhibits 4 and 5 look like the same area of the road that
28   day. I recall that the boy was wearing a dark blue T-shirt and light-colored shorts similar to Exhibits
29   8 and 9.

30   Divindra has finished his/her PhD studies and has returned to India to take a teaching job and to
31   work on his/her thesis. Divindra has no plans to return to the U.S. in the near future.

32   I am deeply sorry about what happened, but there was nothing I could have done to prevent it. I
33   will never forget that horrible moment when the car hit him and I saw him fly through the air. That
34   "whump, thump" sound still haunts me. I'm glad to hear that he is back in school and doing well.

I have read the foregoing deposition and hereby affix my signature that the same is true and correct except as noted herein.

Lynn Snyder

_____
Signature of Deponent

This deposition was taken in the office of plaintiffs' counsel on July 12, *[1 yr ago]*. This deposition was given under oath and was read and signed by the deponent.

Certified by:

Penelope Harrison
Certified Shorthand Reporter
(CSR)

Deposition of
Faridah Z. Goldhammer, PhD

November 27, *[1 yr ago]*

1   I have my doctorate in psychology with a subspecialty in neuropsychology. I received my undergrad-
2   uate degree at New York University and completed my PhD at Columbia University. I work at Children's
3   Hospital in Nita City in the Rehabilitation Department. I was asked to perform an assessment of Sam
4   Scruggs at the request of defense counsel in this matter. I do a small amount of forensic work on a yearly
5   basis, the level of which depends on how busy I am with my regular tasks at Children's Hospital.

6   Sam Scruggs, now a seven-year-old boy from Nita City, Nita, was six years old when he was struck
7   by a car as he attempted to cross over a busy highway. He sustained multiple fractures and a concussion,
8   though the CT scans of his skull and brain were read as normal. He has some retrograde amnesia and
9   did experience loss of consciousness for an unknown period following the impact.

10   Sam lives with both his parents and his older sibling in Nita. This is the first marriage for both
11   parents. He is in the first grade at Horace Mann Elementary in Nita. The question posed to me as an
12   evaluator over one year later is to assess whether or not he has any cognitive residuals as a result of the
13   concussion suffered in this accident.

14   I found Sam to be an attractive, appealing child with an engaging manner. He is extremely polite,
15   friendly, and willing to answer all questions. At times, he would ask me questions that were quite un-
16   related to our discussion about him, the accident, or his life with his family and school. He told stories,
17   asked me questions, but had me repeat some questions so that he could give the best response.

18   In spite of his parents' feeling that Sam is not doing as well following the accident, he appears to have
19   made great strides in moving forward. He certainly does not present the typical issues of Post Traumatic
20   Stress Disorder in spite of his exposure to a traumatic event. He insists that he has no memory of the
21   accident itself and only recalls being taken by the paramedics to Memorial Hospital. He does not have
22   recurring recollections of that day. He talks freely of his hospitalization and can describe in great detail
23   what happened to him. His sleeping is perfect. He used to be scared of things, like the water, but is no
24   longer. He describes being very connected to his various family members and talks with enthusiasm
25   about almost everyone in the family. He is very connected to his parents, who he says have been "very
26   nice" to him since his accident.

27   He thinks school is okay, but "hates reading." When asked how he does in school, he responded,
28   "OK." He has three good friends, Trevor, Luke, and Jim. He likes to go riding on his bicycle with them.
29   He loves watching comedy shows with his family. He also likes watching scary videos. He likes to cel-
30   ebrate birthdays with his extended family.

1   Unlike Sam, I found his parents to be still actively distressed about the events that led to Sam's
2   injuries. They were both tearful, speaking of how the months after Sam was hit were terribly dif-
3   ficult. Both parents feel that Sam is not doing as well as he should be, with diminished impulse
4   control and cognitive ability. They worry about him all the time. They also worry about their ability
5   to be good parents to him following the injury.

6   The testing data performed at Dr. McClaren's direction was available to me, and I reviewed it
7   in detail. In that this was a standard testing battery given to children under these circumstances,
8   it was not necessary for me to repeat this. While Sam sustained a concussion with a brief loss of
9   consciousness, there is no evidence that he has sustained any permanent cognitive impairment. It is
10 significant that the CT scans of his head were interpreted as normal, with no evidence of damage to
11 either his skull or his brain.

12 Though there was undeniable force involved in this accident, with a likely blow to the head, this
13 history, by itself, does not establish injury to the brain. The skull has a broad thickness of bone to
14 help protect brain tissue from the effects of such trauma. There are three surrounding layers of tis-
15 sue inside the skull called the meninges, which also have the same function. In addition, the brain
16 is cushioned by cerebrospinal fluid, which acts as a shock absorber. It would appear that nature's
17 protection mechanisms fulfilled their role admirably in this case.

18 Sam's test scores, both of IQ and basic skills, are in the normal range. The fact that Sam has
19 some impulsivity issues is not indicative of a head injury. It has been well noted by many researchers
20 that the kind of impulsivity that the parents report in Sam is rather typical of children his age. It
21 is difficult, bordering on speculative, to draw any conclusion about a closed head injury in a young
22 child Sam's age. Boys are often slow to develop, though they catch up as time passes. It is just as
23 likely an explanation that hereditary factors are responsible for any delays Sam has experienced.

24 In conclusion, while this was a dramatic accident, the signs and symptoms of head injury are
25 not present at the level it would take to diagnose this condition in Sam. In interviewing his parents,
26 I found them to be hyper-vigilant and anxious about Sam's condition. This is to be expected, given
27 the potential seriousness of what happened. However, it appears to me that the parents' anxiety is
28 driving the diagnosis of a head injury more than anything else. While it may be that Sam can benefit
29 from support services in school, I do not find that this is attributable to the aftereffects of this ac-
30 cident. I have reviewed the Preliminary Care Plan prepared for Sam by the Education Department
31 of the Rehabilitation Center at Memorial Hospital. While I would not argue with much of this if
32 Sam actually had the signs and symptoms of an ongoing impairment resulting from a closed head
33 injury, it is irrelevant given my conclusion that this diagnosis cannot be supported. On the basis of
34 reasonable medical probability, the services enumerated in the Preliminary Care Plan are not neces-
35 sitated by any injury Sam Scruggs sustained in this collision.

I have read the foregoing deposition and hereby affix my signature that the same is true and correct except as noted herein.

Farida J. Goldhammer

Signature of Deponent

This deposition was taken in the office of defendant's counsel on November 27, *[1 yr ago]*. This deposition was given under oath and was read and signed by the deponent.

Certified by:

Penelope Harrison

Penelope Harrison
Certified Shorthand Reporter
(CSR)

DEPOSITION OF
H. JAN MCCLAREN, PHD

November 19, *[1 yr ago]*

1   My name is Dr. H. Jan McClaren. I am a neuropsychologist on the staff of Memorial Hospital. I
2 went to Southern Methodist University as an undergraduate and then graduated from the University
3 of California at San Diego, with a PhD in Psychology, with neuropsychology being my field of study.
4 Since that time, I have become a fully licensed neuropsychologist in the State of Nita and direct the
5 cognitive rehabilitation clinic at Memorial Hospital.

6   I was asked to see Sam Scruggs, a now seven-year-old boy, by Dr. Francis Zindell of Memorial
7 Hospital. At age six, Sam was hit by a car while his family was on vacation at Bayview State Park. He
8 received multiple fractures and a concussion in that event. His orthopedic injuries have healed, leav-
9 ing no residuals. However, a question remains whether he sustained a mild but permanent cognitive
10 impairment as a result of this impact.

11   Sam received no medications following his discharge from the hospital. There are no changes from
12 his past medical history since his discharge. Other than ear infections and some allergies that occasion-
13 ally give him difficulty, Sam has been healthy. He is eating well and sleeping well now, as he has in the
14 past. He has had no seizures. He occasionally complained of some pain in both the right and the left
15 legs in the months following this accident, but none over the last six months. He does not have any
16 definite headaches. He is now able to ambulate independently. He had walking casts placed on each
17 leg, which were removed several weeks after his discharge from the hospital. He is independent in his
18 self-care skills. He does complain of some blurry vision at times, particularly with distance vision and
19 with looking at the board in school. He has some chores that he is responsible for, including feeding
20 the dog, cleaning up his room, and taking out the garbage. His behavior is good, and there are no
21 concerns in this regard. He does sometimes seem to be more fearful and overly cautious than he was
22 prior to his injury, according to his parents report.

23   There have been no changes in Sam's social history. He continues to reside with his parents Pat
24 and Tammy Scruggs, as well as his older sibling Robin. His mother works as an office assistant at
25 Home Loan Bank. His father is employed in the field of heating, ventilation, and air conditioning
26 as a salesman.

27   His parents indicate no developmental milestone delays prior to the injury. There are no other
28 events such as illness or injury prior to the MVA that would reasonably be associated with neurop-
29 sychological deficits. Sam is now halfway through the first grade, reading and generally enjoying
30 school.

1   In my interview with Sam, he indicated that he has no memory of the MVA. There is some retro-
2   grade amnesia for events just prior to the accident, but he is not sure how long. He does not remember
3   the impact or lying by the road afterwards. He most reliably recalled being transported to Memorial
4   Hospital. There were abrasions and swelling to the forehead in the area around the right frontal lobe of
5   the head, indicating likely contact with the road surface in the accident. Subsequent treatment after the
6   casts were removed from his legs primarily consisted of some physical therapy, although this appears
7   to be minimal by his report.

8   Sam's father noted changes in functioning postinjury. Sam was somewhat fatigued for approxi-
9   mately three months. He was not allowed to play sports for a year, although he was very active with
10   soccer prior to his injury. He suffered from headaches, which persisted for approximately four to five
11   months after the MVA. Cognitively, Sam has had difficulty paying attention in school this year in the
12   first grade. It is difficult for him to learn new information, with memory difficulties being reported as
13   the primary cause. Although he has improved in general neurocognitive abilities, his parents do not
14   believe that he has returned to baseline.

15   Sam was administered a battery of psychological and neuropsychological tests. Results indicated a
16   child in the low average range of verbal abilities and in the average range of visuospatial skills. In con-
17   junction with results from academic achievement testing, these data suggest a language-based learning
18   disability with particular difficulties in mathematics and spelling. In contrast, Sam appeared to show
19   adequate attention/concentration on simple tests of cognitive-flexibility, good problem-solving abili-
20   ties, and intact motor and sensory/perceptual functioning. He seemed somewhat slow in acquiring
21   auditorily-presented verbal information, but able to recall most of what he learned after an intermedi-
22   ate delayed interval. No evidence of lateralized cerebral hemispheric impairment or executive dysfunc-
23   tion was inferred from the above data.

24   The brain is a highly sophisticated information-processing center, which has three main structural
25   parts: the cerebellum, the cerebral cortex, and the brain stem. Looking at Exhibit 35, which is a fair
26   and accurate illustration of the human brain and its parts, you can see the exact location of these three
27   main parts. The cerebellum coordinates intricate muscle movements. The cerebral cortex is responsible
28   for complex thought. It is divided into two wrinkled halves, with the surface layer of both hemispheres
29   referred to as the cortex. While it looks the same all over, the cerebral cortex is actually specialized for
30   different functions, depending on location. The brain stem automatically regulates vital life functions
31   such as breathing, heartbeat, and blood pressure.

32   I have seen the brain scans done of Sam not long after the accident at the hospital. I agree that
33   they appear "normal" and show no signs of brain swelling. Nevertheless, other data clearly suggests
34   that Sam did suffer a concussion. He had a head injury. He was unconscious for several minutes and
35   suffers retrograde amnesia. The parents see a marked change in Sam's abilities and behavior, which are
36   confirmed by my tests. A negative brain scan can never be conclusive and can be contraindicated by
37   other data. I think that is the case here.

38   In that the injury to Sam Scruggs' brain likely occurred in the cerebral cortex, I will describe the
39   additional anatomy of that portion. There are four lobes in each hemisphere of the cerebral cortex. As
40   is illustrated by Exhibit 35, the frontal lobes are below the top of the forehead, the parietal lobes on the
41   top, the temporal lobes on the sides, and occipital lobes at the rear.

1   While medical science still is trying to understand many aspects of the brain, the basic functions
2   of each lobe of the cerebral cortex have been identified:
3   • The frontal lobes assist in concentration, planning, judgment, emotional expression, creativity,
4   inhibition, coordinated fine movement, the motor aspects of speech, executive function, social
5   skills, and what we call personality.
6   • The temporal lobes are important for memory, language, and musical awareness.
7   • The parietal lobes involve attention and the interpretation of sensory information.
8   • The occipital lobes perceive and interpret visual input from the eyes.
9   Brain tissue is delicate, with a consistency somewhat like gelatin. While the brain is protected by
10   the thick, bony skull, it is nonetheless susceptible to damage from the application of significant exter-
11   nal force, such as when Sam Scruggs was struck by the car and thrown to the pavement. Immediate
12   injuries result from the physical force inflicted upon the brain, even without penetration from the out-
13   side of Sam's skull through the dura, the tough membrane inside the skull that covers the brain.
14   When the head strikes a solid object, such as Sam hitting the pavement in this case, typically a
15   bruise or contusion occurs in the cortex at the point of contact. It is also possible that there will be
16   another bruise on the opposite side of the brain. These are typically referred to as "coup" and "contra
17   coup" injuries. Such injuries are illustrated on Exhibits 37 and 38, which are fair and accurate depic-
18   tions of these kinds of brain injuries. Sam's head hit with enough force that he was likely to have suf-
19   fered both as shown in Exhibit 38.
20   The force applied to the head and the brain with a sudden acceleration and quick stop also can
21   cause sheering injury to brain tissue. This damages the extensions of the nerve cells called axons, which
22   are physically pulled apart by the force, causing immediate loss of function in the affected neurons.
23   A closed head injury may result in either immediate or delayed symptoms. An immediate symptom
24   was Sam's loss of consciousness following the accident, as well as the concussion and post-concussive
25   syndrome described by his health-care providers in the hospital. Delayed symptoms are the memory and
26   learning problems that have been described in the months since this collision, leading to this evaluation.
27   Memory is controlled deep in the temporal lobes near the center of the brain. The most common
28   type of memory problem following a traumatic brain injury is impaired retrieval of information. This
29   is what my examination and testing of Sam Scruggs revealed, along with compromised learning ability.
30   His brain does not process new information well enough to connect it efficiently to the web of related
31   information. He does remember new information, but not as well as he would have before the brain
32   trauma. Once memory problems of this kind are identified by neuropsychological testing, compensa-
33   tory techniques can be used to help such children better learn new information. The success of these
34   is variable.
35   In summary, Sam has made a remarkable recovery from a rather dramatic accident. However, mild
36   residual neurocognitive impairments were reported in the form of difficulties with attention/concen-
37   tration in new learning. Some support for these complaints was seen in the data obtained from the
38   testing for this evaluation, and it is likely that he has more difficulties in a less structured environment
39   (i.e., situations with multiple distracting stimuli or performing cognitive tasks when fatigued) than the
40   one presented during testing. There is also some evidence that Sam's impulse control and executive
41   function were affected by this head trauma.

1   I am not entirely aware of the type of assistance he receives in school, but it is strongly recom-
2   mended that he be afforded comprehensive services including speech therapy, tutoring, and special
3   accommodations (e.g., extra time taking tests). If these services are not available through his school
4   system, adjunct services may be necessary.

5   It is extremely important that Sam receive these interventions now so that he does not fall behind
6   in the acquisition of academically-mediated skills. This will become even more so as time goes on.
7   Right now, in the early primary grades, Sam is not subject to a particularly academically challenging
8   curriculum. However, this will change rather dramatically in junior high school. Children, such as
9   Sam, who have had head injuries are at a much greater risk of academic failure then. Without con-
10   sistent and effective intervention, they often fall behind in junior high and steadily sink into failure,
11   dropping out before high school graduation.

12   In an effort to avoid this scenario for Sam, I had the Rehabilitation Department of Memorial
13   Hospital prepare a Preliminary Care Plan for him, based on our entire workup here. Our staff is very
14   well qualified and has extensive experience with children who require special assistance as a result of a
15   closed head injury. I have carefully reviewed their Preliminary Care Plan and find, based upon reason-
16   able medical probability, that it is both reasonable and necessary due to the aftereffects of Sam's injuries
17   on July 11, *[2 yrs ago]*.

I have read the foregoing deposition and hereby affix my signature that the same is true and correct
except as noted herein.

H. San McClaren

_____

Signature of Deponent

This deposition was taken in the office of defendant's counsel on November 19, *[1 yr ago]*. This
deposition was given under oath, and was read and signed by the deponent.

Certified by:

Penelope Harrison

_____

Penelope Harrison
Certified Shorthand Reporter
(CSR)

EDUCATION DEPARTMENT DISCHARGE SUMMARY

NAME: Sam Scruggs

DOB: *4-3-[8 yrs ago]*

AGE: 7

DESCRIPTION OF STUDENT

Sam Scruggs is a seven-year-old youth who was hit by a motor vehicle at age six while on a camping trip with his family. He was thrown from the point of impact and had a loss of consciousness of unknown duration. When the paramedics arrived, they found him alert and oriented × 3. He had multiple fractures, including a right femoral and left tibial. In the school year prior to his injury, Sam had completed kindergarten. Sam started the first grade this past fall.

REASON FOR REFERRAL

Sam was referred to this department by Dr. Francis Zindell for neuropsychogical testing as well as evaluation of his academic and cognitive abilities. If indicated, assistance was requested with planning for support services in school.

TEST RESULTS

1. <u>Brigance Inventory of Essential Skills (BIES)</u>

SKILL DESCRIPTION	GRADE EQUIVALENT
Word recognition	1st
Oral recognition	1st
Reading vocabulary	1st
Reading passage comprehension	1st
Sentence memory	> 1st
Listening passage comprehension	1st

NATIONAL INSTITUTE FOR TRIAL ADVOCACY

SKILL DESCRIPTION	GRADE EQUIVALENT
Spelling	> 1st
Sentence writing	> 1st
Computational skills	> 1st
Word problems	1st

2.   Weschler Intelligence Scale For Children III

DESCRIPTION	STANDARD SCORE	PERCENTILE
Verbal IQ	92	30
Performance IQ	104	61
Full scale IQ	97	42
Verbal comprehension index	92	30
Perceptual organization index	110	75
Freedom from distractibility	84	14
Perceptual speed index	101	53

There was a significant difference between Sam's verbal IQ (30th percentile) and his performance IQ (61st percentile).

THE FOLLOWING CONCLUSIONS CAN BE GENERATED FROM ALL THE TEST DATA

Sam clearly has average intelligence. His non-verbal reasoning abilities are stronger than his verbal reasoning skills. He shows some relative weaknesses with verbal comprehension and concentration/distractibility. Difficulties with short-term auditory memory, social judgment, and fine motor speed for copying geometric symbols were also noted. Sam also showed some intra-subtest scatter. For example, on the picture completion subtest, he would miss some of the easier items and then get the more difficult ones correct. The pattern was also noted for both the comprehension and picture arrangement subtests. At times Sam was impulsive, and his fast responding did not always give him a chance to check his responses to see if they were correct. Thus, some mild symptoms related to inattention and impulsivity were also noted qualitatively. His short-term visual memory skills appeared to be intact, scoring at the 60th percentile for visual memory. However, he does show some clear deficits with auditory memory, lower than the 10th percentile. The memory test findings are consistent with the cognitive test findings noted above. He has a mild learning disability in reading and a significant learning disability in the area of written language. More probably than not, this is related to the head trauma sustained in the pedestrian/motor vehicle accident. He does not show any severe symptoms of PTSD. No dreams or nightmares are reported. In fact, there appear to be very few recollections or intrusive thoughts about the accident.

I would like to see school personnel monitor Sam in terms of the ADHD question. My evaluation would indicate that Sam should receive some remedial services by a resource teacher, including individualized tutoring.

H. Jan McClaren, PhD

PRELIMINARY CARE PLAN

NAME: Sam Scruggs

DOB: April 3, *[8 yrs ago]*

DOI: July 11, *[2 yrs ago]*

ITEM	PURPOSE	TIME PERIOD	BASE COST
Neuropsychology evaluation, monitoring, and treatment.	Cognitive and emotional issues related to brain injury.	Current age to life expectancy.	$10,000
Primary care physician evaluation, monitoring, and treatment.	Evaluate, monitor, and treat above and beyond normal needs and provide referrals and monitoring for therapies.	Current age to age 18 (adult needs unknown at this time).	$1,000
Neurologist evaluation, monitoring, and treatment.	Monitor and treat brain injury. Medication management.	Current age to life expectancy.	$20,000
Cognitive rehabilitation.	Develop compensatory strategies in areas of reading, organization, writing, and memory.	Current age to age 21.	$125 per session with an average of 6–8 sessions per year.

NATIONAL INSTITUTE FOR TRIAL ADVOCACY

ITEM	PURPOSE	TIME PERIOD	BASE COST
Individual/family counseling therapy.	To address Sam's needs with adjustment issues related to this accident.	Current age to age 25 (needs beyond unknown at this time).	$100 per session with an estimated 48 sessions minimum required to age 25.
Head CT scans.	Monitor injury sequelae.	Current age to life expectancy.	With contrast: $750–$1,000. Estimated 10 such studies over the course of Sam's life.
Vocational evaluation.	To assist with education planning.	Age 14–18	Average $1,500
Tutoring and supplemental educational resources.	To assist Sam in keeping up in his schoolwork as a result of the brain injury.	Current age to age 18 (adult needs unknown at this time).	$50,000

MEDICAL SUMMARY – SAMUEL SCRUGGS

Report Date: July 3, *[1 yr ago]*

HISTORY OF PRESENT ILLNESS

Sam is a previously healthy seven-year-old male who at age six was struck by a car at high velocity on July 11, *[2 yrs ago]*. He had been camping at Bayview State Park with his family and was hit by a car while running across a busy street. He sustained a brief loss of consciousness of unknown duration along with a right femur fracture and left tib-fib fracture. He was alert and oriented x 3, complaining of pain in both legs, when emergency medical personnel arrived at the scene.

MEDICAL ISSUES

1. Concussion, but CT scan shows no skull fracture. He is currently neurologically stable, but there is a question of whether he sustained a mild closed head injury.

2. Status postmultiple fractures, including right femoral and left tibial, healed without residual disability.

OVERALL FUNCTION

Sam is a delightful boy with a brilliant smile and generally cooperative attitude. He clearly benefits from wonderful family support and presence. His parents report some changes that may be indicative of a mild closed head injury. An appropriate referral will be made for neuropsychological assessment.

Francis J. Zindell, MD

SCRUGGS V. SNYDER — BILLING STATEMENT OF DALE NEWCOMB

SERVICE RENDERED	HOURS/MILES	RATE	AMOUNT
Vehicle inspection	.30	$75.00	$22.50
Travel	1.50	$75.00	$112.50
Visit accident scene w/ assistant; take photos, measurements	6.70	$75.00+ $150.00	$1507.50
Travel	1.50	$150.00	$225.00
Follow-up call— vehicle inspection	.70	$150.00	$105.00
Download and preserve photos	.50	$150.00	$75.00
Mileage	62	$0.45	$27.90
Phone call with client	.20	$75.00	$15.00
Telephone call to police agency	.20	$75.00	$15.00
Download preserved and printout photos off e-mail from client	2.0	$75.00	$150.00
Telephone call to police records custodian	.20	$75.00	$15.00
Request report from State Patrol	.30	$75.00	$22.50
Collision simulator analysis	1.70	$150.00	$255.00
Phone conference with engineering dynamics	.40	$150.00	$60.00

SERVICE RENDERED	HOURS/MILES	RATE	AMOUNT
Phone conference with client	.20	$150.00	$30.00
Phone call re: highway design issue	.20	$150.00	$30.00
Collision speed analysis runs	1.10	$150.00	$165.00
HVE 3 collision simulator dynamics analysis	2.10	$150.00	$315.00
Review depositions of witnesses	3.40	$150.00	$510.00
Review new file data and photos	1.60	$150.00	$240.00
HVE 3 collision dynamics analysis	1.80	$200.00	$360.00
Phone conference with computer animator	.30	$200.00	$60.00
Phone conference with highway design expert	.20	$200.00	$40.00
Phone conference with highway design expert	.20	$200.00	$40.00
Phone conference with computer animator	.20	$200.00	$40.00
Phone conference with computer animator	.20	$200.00	$40.00
Transfer environment from computer animator to HVE simulator	.50	$200.00	$100.00
Review file	.90	$150.00	$135.00

NATIONAL INSTITUTE FOR TRIAL ADVOCACY

SERVICE RENDERED	HOURS/MILES	RATE	AMOUNT
HVE 3 SIMON vehicle dynamics analysis	2.0	$200.00	$400.00
Third computer simulation analysis	1.90	$200.00	$380.00
Graphics preparation	1.20	$200.00	$240.00
Report preparation	1.30	$150.00	$195.00
Review report of defendant's expert	.60	$150.00	$90.00
Research on pedestrian collisions	.70	$150.00	$105.00
Phone conference with client	.20	$150.00	$30.00
Travel, meeting with computer animator re: environment	3.40	$200.00	$680.00
Vehicle pedestrian collision research	.60	$150.00	$90.00
Vehicle pedestrian collision research	.50	$150.00	$75.00
HVE 3 SIMON analysis	1.20	$200.00	$240.00
Phone conference with computer animator	.20	$150.00	$30.00
Phone conference with computer animator	.30	$150.00	$45.00
Download environment for HVE analysis	.90	$150.00	$135.00

SERVICE RENDERED	HOURS/MILES	RATE	AMOUNT
HVE 3 environment preparation	1.80	$200.00	$360.00
HVE 3 environment transfer and preparation	6.0	$200.00	$1,200.00
Set up HVE 3 environment	1.20	$200.00	$240.00
Take file to be copied; delivered to client's office	1.50	$75.00	$112.50
HVE 3 computer analysis	1.10	$200.00	$220.00
HVE 3 computer analysis	1.20	$200.00	$240.00
Scan photos in e-mail	.50	$75.00	$37.50
Additional computer analysis	6.20	$200.00	$1,240.00
Print computer analysis input and output and mail to opposing counsel	.90	$200.00	$180.00
Prepare HVE 3 and video files	1.40	$200.00	$280.00
Phone conference with client	.30	$150.00	$45.00
Prepare additional video files for computer animator and opposing counsel	.30	$200.00	$660.00

SERVICE RENDERED	HOURS/MILES	RATE	AMOUNT
Prepare additional computer analysis and send to animator	1.30	$150.00	$195.00
Review computer analysis and send vehicle specifications to computer animator	1.20	$150.00	$180.00
Phone conference with computer animator	.40	$150.00	$60.00
Review file	.90	$150.00	$135.00
Travel	1.50	$150.00	$225.00
Meeting with client	1.50	$150.00	$225.00
Print photos, research vehicle specs, aid in deposition preparation	1.0	$75.00	$75.00
Deposition preparation	3.90	$150.00	$585.00
Meeting with client	.70	$150.00	$105.00
Obtain new environment for computer animation	1.30	$150.00	$195.00
Review expert reports	1.0	$150.00	$150.00
Vehicle specification research	.60	$150.00	$90.00
Additional computer analysis	2.30	$200.00	$460.00
Additional computer analysis	1.50	$200.00	$300.00
Conference with client	.20	$150.00	$30.00

SERVICE RENDERED	HOURS/MILES	RATE	AMOUNT
Additional computer analysis	2.60	$200.00	$520.00
Review file for deposition	5.0	$150.00	$750.00
Deposition	4.0	$150.00	$600.00
Total	**Hours 97.4** **Miles 62**		**$17,105.40**

EXCERPT FROM *ACCIDENT RECONSTRUCTION PRINCIPLES*
by Louis R. Charles

Page 75: Perception-response time begins when an object or condition for concern enters the driver's visual field, and concludes when the driver develops a conscious awareness that something is present.

Using an appropriate driver reaction time in accident avoidance maneuvers is of critical importance. This is an area where experts frequently move to the extreme corners of the range to prove their point and support their opinion. The reaction times under normal conditions in accident avoidance braking maneuvers range from 1 second to 1.5 seconds.

Given a reasonably clear stimulus and a straightforward situation, there are good data indicating that most drivers, i.e., 85–95 percent, will respond by about 1.5 seconds after first appearance of the object or condition of concern.

The evidence also indicates that the minimum perception-response time for this straightforward situation is about .75 seconds. Thus, the probable range of perception-response times for reasonably straightforward situations should be .75 to about 1.5 seconds. Please note these values are not chiseled in stone on tablets along with other commandments.

EXCERPT FROM *DIAGNOSING CLOSED HEAD INJURIES*
by Wilbert Von Bulow, PhD
(Bigelow Medical Publishing Co. 1995)

Page 2: There are two major classes of head injuries: open, where both the skull and brain are damaged, and closed, where the brain is damaged, but the skull is not. Of the two types, closed head injuries are far more common. They can destroy groups of cells within the brain and disrupt nerve pathways and the integration of different brain processes. The effects are complex and subtle. Mental changes dominate over physical ones. Cognitive and emotional handicaps from closed head injuries can lead to long-term disability.

* * * *

Page 76: The potential effects of a head injury can be placed in three basic areas of impairment:

1. Physical impairment, such as lack of coordination, loss of sensory functions, paralysis, seizures, or headaches;

2. Cognitive impairments affecting memory, attention, concentration, language, and planning and organizing;

3. Psychosocial problems such as irritability, depression, anxiety, and job-related problems.

* * * *

Page 82: Cognitive problems from a head injury can be persistent and chronic, potentially changing the mental capabilities of the patient. The ability to assimilate and process information can be impaired by a closed head injury. Memory defects from whatever cause are difficult to treat.

The usual diagnosis of a head injury case involves the following components:

1. History of head injury and subsequent mental status since the accident.

2. General physical examination.

3. Neurological examination.

4. Radiology studies.

* * * *

Page 89: The problems from head trauma most often missed by medical and psychological examiners fall into the following categories:

NATIONAL INSTITUTE FOR TRIAL ADVOCACY

1. Attentional deficits (e.g., auditory span, fatigue).

2. Subtle memory disorders (e.g., retrieval of old information).

3. Executive dysfunctions (e.g., reduced initiative, problems in planning, poor judgment, reduced self-monitoring).

4. Subtle sensory defects.

There are now hundreds of sophisticated neuropsychological tests that are available for assessing the cognitive function of a patient who has sustained head trauma. However, there are limitations with neuropsychological tests, which may not be able to precisely determine the deficits that follow a head injury. For example, there often is not objective baseline data from prior to the accident with which to compare post-injury test results.

* * * *

Page 92: Seasoned clinical judgment is critical in diagnosing a head injury. The pre-accident function of each patient must be reconstructed and documented to determine whether or not there has been any deterioration following a head trauma. The clinician must attempt to make a reasonable estimate of how well the individual functioned prior to the injury. It involves looking at things such as the individual's prior performance in school and the workplace, as well as the characteristics of interpersonal relationships.

* * * *

Page 96: If a young child is involved, the assessment is more difficult. In such cases, family history should be considered to try to determine if inherited characteristics play any role in the observed deficits.

* * * *

Page 104: The claims process always brings up the question of secondary gain—that is, is the patient pretending to have greater difficulty because of the prospect of compensation from a lawsuit? These are things that the clinician must weigh and rule in or rule out.

NITA GENERAL JURY INSTRUCTIONS

The following jury instructions are intended for use with these materials regardless of whether the trial is in Nita state court or in federal court. In addition, the file contains special instructions dealing with the law applicable in this particular case. The instructions set forth here state general principles that may be applicable in any case and may be used at the discretion of the trial judge.

PART I
PRELIMINARY GENERAL INSTRUCTIONS
GIVEN PRIOR TO THE EVIDENCE

Nita Instruction 1:01   Introduction

You have been selected as jurors and have taken an oath to well and truly try this case. This trial will last one day.

During the progress of the trial there will be periods of time when the Court recesses. During those periods of time, you must not talk about this case among yourselves or with anyone else.

During the trial, do not talk to any of the parties, their lawyers, or any of the witnesses.

If any attempt is made by anyone to talk to you concerning the matters here under consideration, you should immediately report that fact to the Court.

You should keep an open mind. You should not form or express an opinion during the trial and should reach no conclusion in this case until you have heard all of the evidence, the arguments of counsel, and the final instructions as to the law that will be given to you by the Court.

Nita Instruction 1:02   Conduct of the Trial

First, the attorneys will have an opportunity to make opening statements. These statements are not evidence and should be considered only as a preview of what the attorneys expect the evidence will be.

Following the opening statements, witnesses will be called to testify. They will be placed under oath and questioned by the attorneys. Documents and other tangible exhibits may also be received as evidence. If an exhibit is given to you to examine, you should examine it carefully, individually, and without any comment.

National Institute for Trial Advocacy

It is counsel's right and duty to object when testimony or other evidence is being offered that he or she believes is not admissible.

When the Court sustains an objection to a question, you must disregard the question and the answer, if one has been given, and draw no inference from the question or answer or speculate as to what the witness would have said if permitted to answer. You must also disregard evidence stricken from the record.

When the Court sustains an objection to any evidence, you must disregard that evidence.

When the Court overrules an objection to any evidence, you must not give that evidence any more weight than if the objection had not been made.

When the evidence is completed, the attorneys will make final statements. These final statements are not evidence but are given to assist you in evaluating the evidence. The attorneys are also permitted to argue in an attempt to persuade you to a particular verdict. You may accept or reject those arguments as you see fit.

Finally, just before you retire to consider your verdict, I will give you further instructions on the law that applies to this case.

PART II
FINAL GENERAL INSTRUCTIONS

Nita Instruction 2:01   Introduction

Members of the jury, the evidence and arguments in this case have been completed, and I will now instruct you as to the law.

The law applicable to this case is stated in these instructions, and it is your duty to follow all of them. You must not single out certain instructions and disregard others.

Nita Instruction 2:02   Expert Witnesses

You have heard evidence in this case from witnesses who testified as experts. The law allows experts to express an opinion on subjects involving their special knowledge, training and skill, experience, or research. While their opinions are allowed to be given, it is entirely within the province of the jury to determine what weight shall be given to their testimony. You are not bound by the testimony of experts; their testimony is to be weighed as that of any other witness.

Nita Instruction 2:03   Direct and Circumstantial Evidence

The law recognizes two kinds of evidence: direct and circumstantial. Direct evidence proves a fact directly; that is, the evidence by itself, if true, establishes the fact. Circumstantial evidence is the proof of facts or circumstances that give rise to a reasonable inference of other facts; that is, circumstantial evidence proves a fact indirectly in that it follows from other facts or circumstances according to common experience and observations in life. An eyewitness is a common example of direct evidence, while human footprints are circumstantial evidence that a person was present.

The law makes no distinction between direct and circumstantial evidence as to the degree or amount of proof required, and each should be considered according to whatever weight or value it may have. All of the evidence should be considered and evaluated by you in arriving at your verdict.

Nita Instruction 2:04   Burden of Proof

When I say that a party has the burden of proof on any issue, or use the expression "if you find," "if you decide," or "by a preponderance of the evidence," I mean that you must be persuaded from a consideration of all the evidence in the case that the issue in question is more probably true than not true.

Any findings of fact you make must be based on probabilities, not possibilities. It may not be based on surmise, speculation, or conjecture.

Nita Instruction 2:05   Concluding Instruction

The Court did not in any way and does not by these instructions give or intimate any opinions as to what has or has not been proven in the case, or as to what are or are not the facts of the case.

None of these instructions state all of the law applicable, but all of them must be taken, read, and considered together as they are connected with and related to each other as a whole.

You must not be concerned with the wisdom of any rule of law. Regardless of any opinions you may have as to what the law ought to be, it would be a violation of your sworn duty to base a verdict upon any other view of the law than that given in the instructions of the Court.

SPECIFIC INSTRUCTIONS FOR THE SCRUGGS CASE

Nita Instruction 3:01   Claims of Parties

The plaintiffs Tammy and Pat Scruggs, as the guardians of Samuel Scruggs, claim that the defendant was negligent because he/she failed to keep a proper lookout while driving. The plaintiffs claim that defendant's conduct was a proximate cause of the injuries and damages of their ward, Samuel Scruggs. The defendant denies these claims.

The laws of the State of Nita provide that children below the age of seven cannot be held to have been legally negligent no matter how dangerous or reckless their conduct may have been. All the parties to this suit agree that Sam was six years old when he was struck by the defendant's automobile. Therefore, Sam's conduct in running into the road on July 11, *[2 yrs ago]*, may not be considered by you in answering the questions that will be given to you to decide.

However, the defendant does claim that Sam's parents failed to properly supervise their son, causing him to be by a dangerous highway supervised only by his fifteen-year-old sibling, who was playing a ball game. The plaintiffs deny these claims.

The defendant further claims that a non-party to the case, Sam's sibling, Robin Scruggs, failed to properly supervise Sam Scruggs, resulting in his injuries. The plaintiffs deny this claim.

Under the laws of Nita, when a parent places a child into the custody of another person, including another member of the family, that custodian becomes the agent of the parent. This means that, legally, the negligence in the care given the child by the custodian, if any, becomes the negligent conduct of the parent.

The parties have agreed, that is, the plaintiffs do not contest, that Robin Scruggs was the agent of Tammy and Pat Scruggs while he/she was supervising Sam at the ball field. Thus, this is not an issue for you to decide. You should accept Robin's agency as established fact.

Nita Instruction 3:02   Burden of Proof

The plaintiffs have the burden of proving each of the following propositions by a preponderance of the credible evidence:

First, that the defendant acted, or failed to act, in one of the ways claimed by the plaintiffs and that in so acting, or failing to act, the defendant was negligent.

Second, that the negligence of the defendant was a proximate cause of Samuel Scruggs' damages and injuries. "Proximate cause" means an act or omission that, in a natural and continuous sequence, produces an event that would not have occurred without the act or omission. In addition, in order to be a proximate cause, the act or omission complained of must be such that a person using ordinary care would have foreseen that the event, or some similar event, might reasonably be produced thereby.

Third, that the injuries to Samuel Scruggs from being struck by the defendant were as serious and extensive as alleged by the plaintiffs. If, and only if, you find the defendant to have been negligent and a proximate cause of Sam's injuries, you will be asked to determine only one question: regardless of how much fault you place upon the defendant, did Samuel Scruggs suffer the permanent impairment of his learning abilities as a result of being struck by defendant Snyder's car?

To establish the affirmative defense of contributory negligence, the defendant has the burden of proving both of the following propositions by a preponderance of the credible evidence:

First, that plaintiffs Tammy and/or Pat Scruggs and/or non-party Robin Scruggs, as the parents' agent, acted, or failed to act, in one of the ways claimed by the defendant and that in so acting or failing to act, Pat and/or Tammy Scruggs and/or Robin Scruggs was negligent.

Second, that the negligence of the plaintiffs Tammy and/or Pat Scruggs and/or Robin Scruggs was a proximate cause of Samuel Scruggs' damages.

Nita Instruction 3:03   Negligence

"Negligence" is the failure to exercise ordinary care. It is the doing of some act that a reasonably careful person would not do under the same or similar circumstances or the failure to do something that a reasonably careful person would have done under the same or similar circumstances

"Ordinary care" means the care a reasonably careful person would exercise under the same or similar circumstances.

Nita Instruction 3:04   Contributory Negligence

Contributory negligence is negligence, as defined above, on the part of a plaintiff or a third person that is a proximate cause of the injury complained of. If you find contributory negligence, you must determine the degree of negligence, expressed as a percentage, that is attributable to plaintiffs Tammy and Pat Scruggs or Robin Scruggs, as their agent. The Court will furnish you a special verdict form for this purpose. Your answers to the questions in the special verdict form will furnish the basis on which the Court will reduce the amount of any damages you find to have been sustained by the plaintiffs, by the percentage of contributory negligence.

Nita Instruction 3:05   General Duty of Care

Every person has a duty to see the risks of harm to others that could result from their actions or failure to act that would be seen by a person exercising ordinary care.

It is the duty of every person using a public street or highway, whether a pedestrian or a driver of a vehicle, to exercise ordinary care to avoid placing himself or herself or others in danger and to exercise ordinary care to avoid a collision.

Every person using a public street or highway has the right to assume that other persons thereon will use ordinary care and will obey the rules of the road. Every person has a right to proceed on such assumption until he or she knows, or in the exercise of ordinary care should know, to the contrary.

IN THE CIRCUIT COURT OF
DARROW COUNTY, NITA
CIVIL DIVISION

PAT AND TAMMY SCRUGGS, married	)	CIVIL ACTION
persons, as co-guardians of	)	CA 01970
SAMUEL SCRUGGS, a minor,	)	
	)	
Plaintiffs	)	
	)	
v.	)	VERDICT
	)	
LYNN SNYDER,	)	
	)	
Defendant.	)	

VERDICT

We, the jury, make the following answers to the questions submitted by the Court:

QUESTION 1: Was the defendant, Lynn Snyder, negligent as alleged by plaintiffs? Answer Yes or No.

ANSWER: Yes _____ No _____

If you answered No, sign and return this verdict. If you answered Yes, then answer Question 2.

QUESTION 2: Was the negligence of the defendant, Lynn Snyder, a proximate cause of injury or damage to Samuel Scruggs? Answer Yes or No.

ANSWER: Yes _____ No _____

If you answered No, sign and return this verdict. If you answered Yes, then answer Question 3.

NATIONAL INSTITUTE FOR TRIAL ADVOCACY

QUESTION 3: Were either of Sam's parents, Tammy or Pat Scruggs, or his sibling Robin, a non-party for whose conduct the parents were responsible, negligent as alleged by the defendant? Answer Yes or No.

ANSWER: Yes _____ No _____

If you answered Yes, answer Question 4. If you answered No, sign and return this verdict.

QUESTION 4: Was the negligence that you found in answering Question 3 on the part of either of Sam's parents, Tammy or Pat Scruggs, or his sibling Robin, the proximate cause of the damages or injuries to Samuel Scruggs? Answer Yes or No.

ANSWER: Yes _____ No _____

If you answered Yes, answer Question 5. If you answered No, sign and return this verdict.

QUESTION 5: Assume that 100 percent represents the total combined negligence that proximately caused Samuel Scruggs' damages. What percentage, if any, of this 100 percent is attributable to the defendant Lynn Snyder, and the combined effects of Sam's parents and/or his sibling? (Your total must equal 100 percent.)

ANSWER:

PARTIES AND NON-PARTIES	PERCENTAGE
Parents Tammy and Pat Scruggs, including Robin Scruggs	
Defendant Lynn Snyder	
TOTAL	= 100%

Sign and return this verdict.

_____   _____

FOREPERSON'S SIGNATURE   DATE

IN THE CIRCUIT COURT OF
DARROW COUNTY, NITA
CIVIL DIVISION

PAT AND TAMMY SCRUGGS, married	)	CIVIL ACTION
persons, as co-guardians of	)	CA 01970
SAMUEL SCRUGGS, a minor,	)	
	)	
Plaintiffs	)	
	)	
v.	)	VERDICT
	)	
LYNN SNYDER,	)	
	)	
Defendant.	)	

ALTERNATE VERDICT

We, the jury, make the following answers to the questions submitted by the Court:

QUESTION 1: Was the defendant, Lynn Snyder, negligent as alleged by plaintiffs? Answer Yes or No.

ANSWER: Yes _____ No _____

If you answered No, sign and return this verdict. If you answered Yes, then answer Question 2.

QUESTION 2: Was the negligence of the defendant, Lynn Snyder, a proximate cause of injury or damage to Samuel Scruggs? Answer Yes or No.

ANSWER: Yes _____ No _____

If you answered No, sign and return this verdict. If you answered Yes, then answer Question 3.

QUESTION 3: Were either of Sam's parents, Tammy or Pat Scruggs, or his sibling Robin, a non-party for whose conduct the parents were

NATIONAL INSTITUTE FOR TRIAL ADVOCACY

responsible, negligent as alleged by the defendant? Answer Yes or No.

ANSWER: Yes _____ No _____

If you answered Yes, answer Question 4. If you answered No, skip Questions 4 and 5, and answer Question 6.

QUESTION 4: Was the negligence that you found in answering Question 3 on the part of either of Sam's parents, Tammy or Pat Scruggs, or his sibling Robin, the proximate cause of the damages or injuries to Samuel Scruggs? Answer Yes or No.

ANSWER: Yes _____ No _____

If you answered Yes, answer Questions 5 and 6. If you answered No, skip Question 5 and answer Question 6.

QUESTION 5: Assume that 100 percent represents the total combined negligence that proximately caused Samuel Scruggs' damages. What percentage, if any, of this 100 percent is attributable to the defendant Lynn Snyder, and the combined effects of Sam's parents and/or his sibling? (Your total must equal 100 percent.)

ANSWER:

PARTIES AND NON-PARTIES	PERCENTAGE
Parents Tammy and Pat Scruggs, including Robin Scruggs	
Defendant Lynn Snyder	
TOTAL	= 100%

Answer Question 6.

QUESTION 6: Did Samuel Scruggs suffer permanent impairment of his learning abilities as alleged by the plaintiffs as a result of his being struck by defendant Snyder's vehicle? Answer Yes or No.

ANSWER: Yes _____ No _____

Sign and return this verdict.

_____   _____
FOREPERSON'S SIGNATURE   DATE

SECTION II
PROBLEMS

PROBLEM 1

Brainstorming the Video of the Park and Accident Scene

Any case like Scruggs that involves events at a specific location requires a lawyer to take his or her knowledge of the law to that scene to see what facts and circumstances are consistent and inconsistent with the lawyer's current "theory of the case." A visit to the scene imparts a level of comprehension that cannot be obtained by merely reading a report of what happened. It enables the lawyer to think visually, fluidly, and concretely.

Even a video tour of the accident scene, such as you have in this case, can provide the lawyer with an invaluable opportunity to identify facts that support his or her case and anticipate facts that might be used by the opposition.

Look at the video tour of Bayview State Park on the DVD that accompanies the case file. Look at it with a plaintiff or defense lawyer's critical eye. Identify the three best arguments or factual theories for your client that can be made on the basis of what you see in the video. At the same time, anticipate the three best arguments or factual theories that could be made for your opponent's position based upon what is shown in this video. Try to come up with a response to each one of them. After all, what is depicted in the video are "hard facts" that must fit any favorable theory of "what happened." This will likely require more than one viewing.

The scenes in the video go by quickly. You may want to slow down the motion or stop it entirely. Are there any portions of the video tour that you want to slow down or stop? What are they? Why do you want to stop the video at that point? Should you also do this for the jury? Why? Be prepared to discuss this in class.

A basic tenet of Gestalt Psychology is that the whole is greater than the sum of its parts. Combinations of words and pictures, as well as multiple images, can increase the comprehension and effectiveness of visual evidence. Can you think of any other evidence in this case file that you can combine with the video tour that may increase the jury's comprehension of the facts and enhance the video's persuasive power? What is it? How would you meld it together in your courtroom presentation?

Prepare a list of the favorable facts shown in the video and explain why they help your theory of what happened. Prepare a list of the unfavorable facts and explain why they hurt your theory of the case. Write out the three best arguments that you and your opponent can derive from the video and tell how you will either counter or fit the unfavorable facts into your theory or theories of the case. Be prepared to discuss these matters in class. Finally, be prepared to discuss how you will use the video at trial and what other exhibits or testimony will accompany its presentation at trial.

PROBLEM 2

Motion Practice

The Defense has filed a motion to exclude the computer simulations of Dale Newcomb on the ground that they are irrelevant, unreliable, speculative, and unduly prejudicial. Counsel will participate in a mock hearing. Each side will be allowed five minutes to present their arguments. You should prepare an outline of your basic points, focusing on factual arguments applied to your general knowledge of the rules of evidence.

For the Defense, argue in favor of your motion with regard to:

    a. The simulation of the accident

    b. Feasibility Study No. 1

    c. Feasibility Study No. 2

Plaintiffs' counsel, oppose the defense motion.

PROBLEM 3

Brainstorming the Video of the Focus Group

For many years fields such as marketing, brand identity, and politics have used focus groups to identify the range of responses to products or the positions of candidates for public office. Comparatively recently, lawyers have adapted this technique to try and predict how lay jurors will react to the facts and arguments in pending cases. Among other things, focus groups can help to establish profiles of jurors likely to be either favorably or unfavorably disposed toward the position of any given party to a lawsuit. Some of the variables include age, gender, ethnicity, education, marital status, parenthood, employment, and income level. Focus groups can also help lawyers identify "hot button" issues, as well as how to best phrase these for maximum juror appeal.

Based on your own life's experience, put together profiles of jurors likely to be for and against your position in this case. Then watch the focus group video and compare how the reactions of the individual members of this group compare to your predictions. Did any of the views of the focus group members come as a surprise to you? Why? Was there any way you could have predicted these views based on the demographic information provided initially? Have you changed any of your ideas about themes, approach, and argument in this case as a result of what you have learned from this focus group? Does the application of focus groups to legal cases seem like a useful advocacy technique based on what you have seen?

[Note that this focus group considered an earlier version of the facts, in which there was a significantly lower alcohol consumption by Lynn Snyder and where Snyder did not admit to being on the phone. Also, the focus group was asked to determine what, if any, award should be made to Scruggs for his physical injuries and future damages.]

PROBLEM 4

Voir Dire

Following these Problems is a Juror Information Form. Those playing the potential jurors (venire) should complete the form and give it to those who are conducting the voir dire. The jurors are to assume the name and persona of someone they know well, such as a relative or friend, but who is not a lawyer or law student. Jurors should *not* assume the personality of a person who is extremely peculiar or abnormal.

Part A: For the Plaintiffs, conduct at least a ten minute voir dire of the venire. Pick at least three issues you feel you must address in this case. Assume that damages are not in issue at the trial.

Part B: Same assignment as Part A, but assume that damages, as well as liability, are in issue at the trial.

Part C: For the Defense, conduct at least a ten minute voir dire of the venire. Follow up on the issues raised by Plaintiffs' counsel. Be prepared to question on at least three issues that you feel must be addressed by you in this case. Assume the trial is only on liability.

Part D: Same assignment as Part C, but assume that damages and liability are in issue at the trial.

Problem 5

Opening Statement

Part A: For the Plaintiffs, deliver a _____ minute opening statement to the jury. Assume that the only issue at trial is liability, not damages.

Part B: For the Plaintiffs, deliver a _____ minute opening statement to the jury on the issue of the Plaintiffs' damages, not liability.

Part C: For the Plaintiffs, deliver a _____ minute opening statement on both the liability and damages issues.

Part D: For the Defense, deliver a _____ minute opening statement to the jury. Assume that the only issue at trial is liability, not damages.

Part E: For the Defense, deliver a _____ minute opening statement to the jury on the issue of the Plaintiffs' damages only, not liability.

Part F: For the Defense, deliver a _____ minute opening statement on both the liability and damages issues.

For purposes of the following Exhibit Assignments, Problems 5–10, do not conduct an entire direct examination of the witnesses. Limit your direct to the questions that are necessary for the exhibit to be admissible, and then offer the exhibit into evidence. Counsel for both sides must be prepared to raise and meet all possible, legitimate evidentiary objections.

PROBLEM 6

Exhibits: Photos

For the Plaintiffs, lay the necessary foundation to admit the photos taken at the accident scene. You can use any of the witnesses listed in the case file who you feel are necessary. You may invent witnesses that are not mentioned in the case file.

Defense counsel, oppose the offers.

PROBLEM 7

Exhibits: Clothing

Part A: For the Defense, lay the necessary foundation to admit the T-shirt and shorts worn by Sam when he was hit by Snyder's car. Absent real clothing, assume that the photos are the actual articles of clothing. You can use any witness or witnesses you feel are necessary. You may invent witnesses that are not mentioned in the case file.

Plaintiffs' counsel, oppose the offers.

Part B: For the Defense, lay the necessary foundation to admit the photos of the T-shirt and shorts worn by Sam when he was hit. Assume that the clothing is not available.

Plaintiffs' counsel, oppose the offers.

PROBLEM 8

Exhibits: Diagrams

For the Plaintiffs, introduce the two diagrams illustrating the skid marks of Flyberg's and Snyder's vehicles. Use any necessary witness(es).

Defense counsel, oppose the offer, if possible.

Problem 9

Exhibits: Stop-Action Photos

For the Defense, introduce Trooper Fielder's stop-action photographs of the scene of the accident. Plaintiffs' counsel, oppose the offer.

Problem 10

Exhibits: Photo of Underpass Sign

For the Defense, introduce the photographs of the campground signs pointing to the underpass. Use any necessary witness(es).

Plaintiffs' counsel, oppose the offer, if possible.

Problem 11

Exhibits: Video of Campsite and Accident Scene

Plaintiffs' counsel, introduce the video walk through of the park and the accident scene.

Part A: Assume that the video was taken by you personally. Use any necessary witness(es) to admit the recording.

Part B: Assume that the video was recorded by your investigator, Paul Drake, approximately one year after the accident.

Defense counsel, oppose the offers, if possible.

Problem 12

Direct and Cross-Examination of Plaintiffs' Witness without Exhibits

For the Plaintiffs, conduct the direct examination, *without the aid of any of the exhibits in the file,* of your assigned witness from the following:

    a. Chris Buck

    b. Alex Flyberg

    c. Robin Scruggs

    d. Pat Scruggs

For the Defense, cross-examine.

Problem 13

Direct and Cross-Examination of Plaintiffs' Witness with Exhibits

Part A: For the Plaintiffs, conduct the direct examination, *with the aid of any of the exhibits in the file,* of your assigned witness from the following:

    a. Chris Buck

    b. Alex Flyberg

    c. Robin Scruggs

    d. Pat Scruggs

Assume any exhibits you use have not been admitted into evidence yet.

Part B: For the Plaintiffs, same assignment as Part A except assume that any exhibits you use have already been admitted into evidence.

For the Defense, cross-examine, with the same assumption Plaintiffs' counsel was instructed to follow for each part.

PROBLEM 14

Direct and Cross-Examination of Defense's Witness without Exhibits

For the Defense, conduct the direct examination, *without the aid of any of the exhibits,* of your assigned witness from the following:

   a. Jan Moriarity
   b. Trooper Sandy Fielder
   c. Lynn Snyder

Plaintiffs' counsel, cross-examine.

PROBLEM 15

Direct and Cross-Examination of Defense's Witness with Exhibits

Part A: For the Defense, conduct the direct examination, *with the aid of any of the exhibits,* of your assigned witness from the following:

   a. Jan Moriarity
   b. Trooper Sandy Fielder
   c. Lynn Snyder

Assume any exhibits you use have *not* been admitted into evidence yet.

Part B: For the Defense, same assignment as Part A except assume that any exhibits you use have already been admitted into evidence.

Plaintiffs' counsel, cross-examine with the same assumption Defense counsel was instructed to follow for each part.

PROBLEM 16

Expert Examination

Part A: For the Plaintiffs, conduct the direction examination of your assigned expert witness from the following:

    a. Dale Newcomb

    b. Dr. McClaren

Defense counsel, cross-examine.

Part B: For the Defense, conduct the direct examination of Dr. Goldhammer.

Plaintiffs' counsel, cross-examine.

For the purposes of these Impeachment Problems, do not conduct an entire cross-examination of the witness. Confine your examination to the impeachment of the witness with his or her prior inconsistent statement.

PROBLEM 17

Impeachment: Lynn Snyder

Part A: Assume that on direct examination defendant Lynn Snyder testified, *"I had only one drink—I think it was a light beer—at brunch the morning of the accident."*

For the Plaintiffs, impeach Snyder's direct testimony with his/her deposition.

Defense counsel, rehabilitate the witness.

Part B: Assume that on direct, Snyder testified, *"I gave my cell phone to Divindra Patel a couple of minutes before the accident so Divindra could find out if there was a later flight to Boston that day."*

For the Plaintiffs, impeach Snyder's direct testimony with his/her deposition.

Defense counsel, rehabilitate the witness.

Part C: Assume that at the scene, approximately forty-five minutes after the accident, Snyder gave Trooper Fielder a signed hand written statement describing the accident that reads:

> *I never saw the kid I hit until he was directly in front of my car when it was too late to avoid hitting him.*

Assume further that on direct examination Snyder testified in accordance with his/her deposition testimony.

For the Plaintiffs, impeach Snyder's direct testimony.

Defense counsel, rehabilitate the witness.

Part D: Assume that on direct, Snyder testified in accordance with his/her deposition testimony. Assume that prior to trial, Snyder was interviewed by Plaintiffs' counsel's investigator, Paul Drake, at Snyder's apartment. Drake took notes of his interview and returned two days later with a typed statement for Snyder to sign. After reading the statement, Snyder made and initialed a correction in his/her handwriting, as shown below. The statement included the following text:

> *north – LS*
> I was headed ~~south~~ on the coastal highway headed toward the Nita City Airport. . . . When I saw the boy standing on the other side of the road near the edge, I instinctively took my foot off the gas and moved it over the brake, but not touching it. You never know what kids will do.

For the Plaintiffs, impeach Snyder's direct testimony.

Defense counsel, rehabilitate the witness.

Problem 18

Impeachment: Chris Buck

Part A: Assume that on direct Chris Buck testified, "When the boy reached the centerline, I could tell that the on-coming Kia didn't notice him. I could see clearly that the driver was talking on a cell phone."

Defense counsel, impeach Buck's testimony with his/her deposition.

Plaintiffs' counsel, rehabilitate the witness.

Part B: Assume that on direct, Buck testified as stated in Part A. Assume that the deposition of Buck is a typed and signed statement of Buck given to an adjuster from Snyder's auto insurance company.

Defense counsel, impeach Bucks testimony with the statement to the insurance adjuster.

Plaintiffs' counsel, rehabilitate the witness.

Problem 19

Impeachment: Robin Scruggs

Assume that on direct examination, Robin Scruggs testified, "When the ranger decided to let the big kids, like me and Jessica, play softball too, Sam began sulking and asked if he could return to our campsite. I said he could but that he must use the underpass. He said, 'OK. I promise,' and walked down the steps toward the underpass."

For the Defense, impeach Robin with her/his deposition.

Plaintiffs' counsel, rehabilitate the witness.

PROBLEM 20

Closing Argument

Assume liability, not damages, is in issue:

Part A: Present a _____ minute summation for the Plaintiffs.

Part B: Present a _____ minute summation for the Defense.

Assume damages, not liability, are in issue:

Part C: Present a _____ minute summation for the Plaintiffs.

Part D: Present a _____ minute summation for the Defense.

Assume both damages and liability are in issue:

Part E: Present a _____ minute summation for the Plaintiffs.

Part F: Present a _____ minute summation for the Defense.

NITA JUROR INFORMATION FORM

_____   _____   _____   _____

Name   Date of Birth   Age   Place of Birth

Marital Status: Number of children:

__ Married __ Single __ Separated __ Divorced   ___ Male ___ Female

_____   _____   _____

Occupation   Employer   Length of Employment

_____   _____   _____

Spouse's Occupation   Spouse's Employer   Length of Employment

_____   _____

Length of residence in this county   Religious affiliation or preference

Have you ever served on a civil jury?   Have you ever served on a criminal jury?

___ Yes ___ No   ___ Yes ___ No

If yes, how many times?   If yes, how many times?
_____   _____

Have you ever been a party to a lawsuit?   Have you or any member of your family
                                               been a peace officer?
___ Yes ___ No
                                               ___ Yes ___ No

If yes, what kind?

_____

If yes, how many times?

_____

NATIONAL INSTITUTE FOR TRIAL ADVOCACY